# THE K-WAVE ON-SCR|

*The K-Wave On-Screen* provides an engaging and accessible exploration of the meaning of *K-* through the lens of words and objects in K-dramas and K-films.

Once a small subculture known only to South Korea's East Asian neighbours, the Korean Wave has exploded in popularity around the globe in the last decade. Its success has been fuelled by social media and the advanced technological capabilities of South Korea. With #KpopTwitter having amassed 7.8 billion tweets and with K-films receiving acclaim from major award ceremonies, the K-Wave is now a global cultural phenomenon. This book touches on globally popular productions, such as *Parasite* (2019), *Squid Game* (2021), *Pachinko* (2022), *SKY Castle* (2018), and *Kim Ji-young: Born 1982* (2019) to highlight that *K-* has departed from the traditional meaning of 'Korean-ness' to become a new, globally informed, and hybrid entity.

This book will be of interest to students in East Asian studies, and those engaged with Korean language learning. The book will also appeal to those interested in Korean culture and media.

**Jieun Kiaer** is the Young Bin Min-Korea Foundation Professor of Korean Linguistics at the Faculty of Asian and Middle Eastern Studies, and Senior Research Fellow and Dean of Degrees at Hertford College, University of Oxford.

**Emily Lord**, MSt., is a Faculty Research Specialist at the Applied Research Laboratory for Intelligence and Security, University of Maryland.

**Loli Kim** is a Postdoctoral Researcher on the Leverhulme Haenyeo project at the Faculty of Asian and Middle Eastern Studies, University of Oxford.

# Routledge Studies in East Asian Translation

Series Editors: Jieun Kiaer, *University of Oxford, UK*
Amy Xiaofan Li, *University College London, UK*

*Routledge Studies in East Asian Translation* aims to discuss issues and challenges involved in translation between Chinese, Japanese and Korean as well as from these languages into European languages with an eye to comparing the cultures of translation within East Asia and tracking some of their complex interrelationships.

Most translation theories are built on translation between European languages, with only few exceptions. However, this Eurocentric view on language and translation can be seriously limited in explaining the translation of non-European literature and scholarship, especially when it comes to translating languages outside the Indo-European family that have radically different script forms and grammatical categories, and may also be embedded in very different writing traditions and cultures. This series considers possible paradigm shifts in translation theory, arguing that translation theory and practice need to go beyond European languages and encompass a wider range of literature and scholarship.

**Loanwords and Japanese Identity**
Inundating or Absorbed?
*Naoko Hosokawa*

**The Language of Hallyu**
More than Polite
*Jieun Kiaer*

**The K-Wave On-Screen**
In Words and Objects
*Jieun Kiaer, Emily Lord, and Loli Kim*

For more information about this series, please visit: www.routledge.com/ Routledge-Studies-in-East-Asian-Translation/book-series/RSEAT

# THE K-WAVE ON-SCREEN

## In Words and Objects

*Jieun Kiaer, Emily Lord, and Loli Kim*

LONDON AND NEW YORK

Designed cover image: CJNattanai via Getty Images

First published 2024
by Routledge
4 Park Square, Milton Park, Abingdon, Oxon OX14 4RN

and by Routledge
605 Third Avenue, New York, NY 10158

*Routledge is an imprint of the Taylor & Francis Group, an informa business*

© 2024 Jieun Kiaer, Emily Lord and Loli Kim

*British Library Cataloguing-in-Publication Data*
A catalogue record for this book is available from the British Library

*Library of Congress Cataloging-in-Publication Data*
Names: Kiaer, Jieun, author. | Lord, Emily (Linguist), author. | Kim, Loli, author.
Title: The K-wave on-screen : in words and objects / Jieun Kiaer, Emily Lord, Loli Kim.
Description: Abingdon, Oxon ; New York, NY : Routledge, 2024. | Series: Routledge
    studies in East Asian translation | Includes bibliographical references and index.
Identifiers: LCCN 2023005276 (print) | LCCN 2023005277 (ebook) |
    ISBN 9781032066530 (hardback) | ISBN 9781032066516 (paperback) |
    ISBN 9781003203230 (ebook)
Subjects: LCSH: Television programs—Korea (South)—History—21st century. |
    Motion pictures—Korea (South)—History—21st century. | Popular culture—Korea
    (South)—History—21st century.
Classification: LCC PN1992.3.K6 K53 2024 (print) | LCC PN1992.3.K6 (ebook) |
    DDC 791.45095195—dc23/eng/2023-03-13
LC record available at https://lccn.loc.gov/2023005276
LC ebook record available at https://lccn.loc.gov/2023005277

ISBN: 978-1-032-06653-0 (hbk)
ISBN: 978-1-032-06651-6 (pbk)
ISBN: 978-1-003-20323-0 (ebk)

DOI: 10.4324/9781003203230

Typeset in Times New Roman
by Apex CoVantage, LLC

# CONTENTS

# FIGURES

# TABLES

# ACKNOWLEDGEMENTS

We would first like to thank our amazing Editorial Assistant Iola Ashby at Rout-ledge for her ongoing patience and assistance in the creation of this book. We would also like to give a huge thanks to all our colleagues at the Faculty of Asian and Middle Eastern Studies at Oxford. Jieun Kiaer would like to thank Louise Hossien and Simon Barnes-Sadler for their feedback and editorial help. Jieun also wishes to express thanks to the Korea Foundation for supporting her fieldwork in 2021. Emily Lord would like to thank her husband, Robert, for his support through-out the writing of this book. Loli Kim would like to thank her husband for his support, and her colleagues at the Faculty of Asian and Middle Eastern Studies at Oxford, whose discussions contribute to every single project.

This work was supported by the Core University Program for Korean Studies of the Ministry of Education of the Republic of Korea and Korean Studies Promotion Service at the Academy of Korean Studies (AKS-2021-OLU-2250004).

# PRELIMS

In this book we have used the Revised Romanisation system when romanising Korean *hangeul*, which was developed by the National Academy of Korean language and is the official romanisation system used in Korea. Every first use of a Korean word we present with romanised Korean first (italicised), followed by the *hangeul* form of the word in brackets, followed by the English translation in single quotation marks. On every mention afterwards we use the romanised Korean word, or in the case of film titles the English title. In image captions, following the complete entry of the film in all Korean and English forms, we simply refer to the film's English title. In the main text, a film title will only be followed by its year of release the first time it is mentioned in a given chapter and following this the year will not be mentioned again unless it was felt necessary for the sake of distinguishing between titles, until the next chapter. In Korean tradition, when we refer to Korean people, we arrange the names with the surname followed by the first, unless the person has chosen to follow a Western format. On a final note, for an overview of all the media sources in this book, please refer to Appendix 1, which includes all sources.

# 1

# DEFINING *K-*

FIGURE 1.1 The 2022 *Hallyu! The Korean Wave* exhibition at the Victoria & Albert (V&A) Museum in South Kensington, London.

We begin this book of words and objects with the Victoria & Albert (V&A) Museum's poster for its 2022 *Hallyu! The Korean Wave* exhibition[1] (Figure 1.1). The poster tells us a lot about what the Korean Wave – or K-Wave – is, and how it is impacting on society beyond Korea. Notice how in the poster there are three forms of the term 'Korean Wave': there is "한류", which is the Korean word printed in *hangeul*. This is presented first and largest of all; then there is the romanised form of the word "*Hallyu*"; and lastly the English form is the "Korean Wave". If we consider the target audience being predominantly Anglophone, since the poster's location is in London, we might ask why all three forms are used together and why in this order. Usually, translations are favourable to ensure understanding among the target market, which is non-Koreans. Also, while London's inhabitants and visitors have diverse cultures and languages, with the K-Wave arising only three decades ago in the 1990s, we must ask how many of these are going to be Korean speakers. Indeed, it is likely that the majority will not

DOI: 10.4324/9781003203230-1

be. This points to an assumption made by the V&A Museum that *hangeul* is symbolic of the K-Wave, and enough so that it is as impactful as any English header.

This isn't the first time that we have seen *hangeul* being given a prominent position on signage in a predominantly Anglophone environment. In London, the popular restaurant *Bunsik* 분식 provides another instance of using both *hangeul* and romanised Korean (Figure 1.2). Like the V&A Museum poster, a single word is presented in multiple ways; each creates another dimension of meaning that grants or restricts access to meanings relating to Korea or the K-Wave, depending upon who is interpreting. This is precisely why we have opened with this object because it exhibits the multidimensional and transnational nature of *K-*; it can and does cross the boundaries typically formed by language and culture, while simultaneously embodying traditional aspects of them too. When the K-fandom come across the signage *Bunsik* 분식, for instance, the *hangeul* serves as a beacon of the K-Wave, blaring "K-Wave!" even if not spelt out explicitly in English. Romanised Korean has a similar effect when read aloud by those familiar with the sounds of the language. It has dynamic connotations to the music of K-pop bands, such as *BTS* and *Blackpink*; to television shows, like *Ojingeo Geim* (오징어 게임) 'Squid Game' (2021), *Binsenjo* (빈센조) 'Vincenzo' (2021), and *All of Us Are Dead* (2022); as well as to Korean foods popularised by the K-Wave. Indeed, the 'multifacetedness' of the K-Wave is part of what seems to be transmitted by the sounds of Korean.

FIGURE 1.2   Exterior view of the *Bunsik* 분식 restaurant in London.

In comparison, Koreans who come across *Bunsik* 분식 view it in an entirely different way. *Bunsik* is their local snack food culture, so it is entwined in their identity. It doesn't spark Koreans' curiosity in the same way, nor does it feel like engaging in a trend to them. Rather, it is a means of connecting with their homeland while they're away from it. *Bunsik* (분식) literally means 'food made from flour', using flour as a reference to snacks rather than main meals, which are traditionally rice based, rather than wheat based, and so bear the association of being a snack. The foods themselves are not all made from only flour, though. Popular *bunsik* include snack foods like *ddeokbokki* (떡볶이) 'spicy rice cakes', and *eomuk* (어묵) 'Korean fish cake', and *gimbap* (김밥) 'meat and/or vegetables wrapped in rice and seaweed paper'. *Bunsik* is not considered high-end in Korea, but rather cheap and cheerful. These foods are sold at markets and by street food vendors, often near to tourist attractions and in shopping districts. *Bunsik* 분식, however, is not cheap and cheerful like its Korean counterpart, and not what Koreans expect when they enter.

*Bunsik* 분식 was designed to communicate a trendy London version of *bunsik* to K-Wave consumers, which is another dimension of *K*-. Koreans, however, would see *Bunsik* 분식 as a way to connect with their roots. The same goes for the V&A Museum's *Hallyu! The Korean Wave* exhibition: for Koreans it provides a chance to connect with their traditional culture and identity, rather than solely with Korean popular culture, which many foreign fans may associate synonymously with one another.

These different dimensions of interpretation and engagement are dynamic, subjective, and as such tricky to pin down, yet their existence is unarguable. The success of Korean content has largely been the result of this multidimensionality, because the traditional and contemporary dimensions of K-culture provide both curiosity (from the former) and universality in the hybridity (from the latter). For instance, in K-dramas, we see the familiar ups and downs of life, yet they are presented in a new 'Korean' way. There are components that allow us to comprehend what's happening, and components that we discover for the first time. Then, there is the gap in translation, and subsequent variety In viewer interpretation; this snowballs in the semiotic productivity among fans that results from translation, which also has an impact on commercial industries of the K-Wave, and that in turn generates further curiosity.

This capacity for multidimensional engagement is precisely what defines *K*- or 'K-ness', giving the power to *hangeul* so that it could be used effectively on the header of the V&A Museum's poster. *K*- and *Korean* are indeed not the same, even though *K*- does contain elements of Korean culture. Just like how *K-Wave* and *Hallyu* signify Korean popular culture's popularity in non-Korean territories, rather than Korean popular culture itself, *K*- signifies something translingual and transcultural. It is an amalgamation of Korean traditional culture with Western culture and other modern trends, which all began with the Korean government's goal to globalise Korean popular culture. The *Oxford English Dictionary* even defines *K*- as an adjective, separate from the word 'Korean', rather than simply an abbreviation of it, which is added to English nouns that relate to Korean (popular) culture (e.g., "K-beauty, K-culture, K-food, K-style, etc.").

*Loli:*   I recently saw a *Chingu* 'friend' t-shirt that is a perfect example of the hybridity, and specifically the hybridity born from snowballing, and heavily influenced by Western fandom. The typeface, punctuation, and colour scheme are taken from the famous US sitcom *Friends* (1994–2004). This combination creates a powerful multimodal intertext that is recognisable to many due to the success of *Friends* in Western popular culture. The word 'friends' is, however, replaced with the Korean word for 'friend', *chingu*, and the t-shirt reads 'C·H·I·N·G·U' instead of 'F·R·I·E·N·D·S'. The Korean word *chingu* is not even plural, it's singular, simply meaning 'friend'. However, the word has been popularised through Korean popular culture, and along with the power of *Friends* logo symbolism, the play on words and popular culture content can be comprehended without entirely equalising the translation. Participation is the primary goal, and products like these let the K-fandom participate in the K-Wave, whilst also retaining some of their own identity. The K-Wave has been – be it commercially or through the fandom – persistent in this form of hybridity that maximises on the solidarity of fans; in this case the solidarity of both *Friends* and K-Wave fans.

Hybridity appeals to the millennials because for them (and the generations that follow) hybridity is the norm, with one in five people speaking a second language. For these consumers, *K-* is inclusive, relatable, and natural. Further, this hybridity is increasingly formalised, with institutions like the *Oxford English Dictionary* adding twenty-six Korean words to the English language, and with hybrid as well as traditional definitions. Words like *oppa*, which has a hierarchical implication in its traditional Korean use, meaning 'older brother', is used by fandom to mean 'handsome guy' or 'boyfriend' (Figure 1.3).

*Chimaek* and *mukbang* are further examples. *Chimaek*, for example, is a combination of the English word 'chicken' and part of the Korean word for beer,

FIGURE 1.3   The family-friend tree of address terms.

'*maekju*'. These are hybrid words that describe elements of K-popular food culture, but it is through engagement with other cultures that this concept could evolve. Then, there are Korean foods that are emerging directly from Western culinary contexts rather than being adopted from Korean ones; snowballing is indeed multifaceted. UK branches of the popular chicken takeaway restaurant *KFC*, for instance, recently released the "Korean BBQ wrap". UK branches of Costco recently released a similar product at the store's café, though this is called a "Korean BBQ Bake". In UK supermarkets, "Korean" products have been released by brands that are not known to produce Korean products. One example is *Cauldron*, which recently released a snack food called "Korean Bites" that is similar to the Middle Eastern food, kofta. It does not remotely resemble traditional Korean food.

Mainstream organisations then add to this by providing recipes and articles. BBC Good Food released its own recipe for *dalgona coffee*,[2] a trending food inspired by the brown sugar biscuit *popgi*, which was reconceptualised as '*dalgona*' and popularised by the hit Netflix show, *Squid Game* (2021). *Dalgona* coffee isn't traditionally Korean either, nor is the word '*dalgona*' even Korean but rather a collaboration between popular culture, fandom, and the media that has snowballed into something new – something *K-*.

Noticeably, many of the products are financially accessible, just like the *K-* they access on-screen, despite the luxurious aesthetic often associated with Korea as created by Samsung and LG, demonstrating that Korea is technologically advanced and well off. It all basically amounts to a masterful rebranding of Korea as a cosmopolitan utopia within anyone's grasp. *BBC Good Food*, for instance, describes their *dalgona coffee* recipe as an "easy whipped coffee recipe" that takes only 8 minutes to prepare and needs 3 tablespoons of instant coffee, 2 tablespoons of sugar, and 400–500 ml of milk.

This is perhaps why it has been even easier for *K-* to snowball. For instance, *dalgona coffee's simple tasty recipe* snowballed, and now there are vegan *matcha dalgona coffee* recipes,[3] *matcha dalgona coffee* recipes,[4] *dalgona latte* recipes,[5] *strawberry dalgona* recipes,[6] and popular YouTube vloggers demonstrating how to make diverse varieties of *dalgona coffee*.[7]

Dalgona has also snowballed terminologically, with the term 'whipped coffee' becoming synonymous and often interchangeable with '*dalgona*', even though *dalgona* is a word used to describe the Korean brown sugar treat *popgi* in *Squid Game* within the dimension of *K-* and does not mean 'whipped'. *Dalgona* is somewhat mysterious in this respect. Their popularity, however, is very clear. For example, *The Happy Noona's* (64,100 subscribers) 'How to Make Dalgona Coffee/Frothy Coffee'[8] video had more than 10 million views on YouTube.

*K-* has developed a 'soft power' that is practically paradoxical, as it is much more than simply a phase of popular culture. K-fandom, for instance, even wield their number and solidarity politically.[9] The K-Wave has moved beyond being merely a wave of popular culture (or 'low culture') to influencing 'high culture'.

FIGURE 1.4 The 'finger heart' gesture. Image created by Loli Kim.

As well as verbal language, like the Korean words added to the *Oxford English Dictionary*, the K-Wave is impacting non-verbal gestures, and culture too. The famous 'finger heart' hand gesture (Figure 1.4) is an excellent example. It is a widely known gesture often used as a pose when being photographed but also used as an indicator of the K-Wave in foreign communication with Koreans. When President Biden posed with K-pop band BTS during their visit to the White House as UN ambassadors to discuss Asian Hate in 2022, he made a finger heart gesture. In other instances, the finger heart is used as an expression of solidarity amongst K-fans.

## De-Westernised and de-colonised discourses

By presenting a lucrative model for transnationalism, transculturalism, and translingualism, the K-Wave is impacting more than just popular culture flows. Its promotion of non-Eurocentric perspectives has introduced a de-Westernised and de-colonised discourse.[10] This, in turn, has given way to and supported a desire for authentic Korean content, rather than the mere accessibility of K-content, among foreign viewers. This has been demonstrated in the interest shown by viewers in understanding what's really happening in K-films and K-dramas beyond the subtitles.[11,12]

De-Westernised discourses serve as models for bridge-building across disparities within industries and societies, reaching even those who don't actively engage with *K-*. This often occurs second-hand, in verbal and visual footage from K-content that leaks into other things (like *Squid Game* themes on Roblox and TikTok). Schoolchildren, for example, who are not old enough to watch the show, engage with components of the show through these platforms. Costumes, games, phrases, and foods then enter these children's homes, and the same is true for adults. The overall implication here is that other marginalised cultures can potentially export their cultural projects successfully too.

## Agency of K-fandom

As a result of de-Westernised and de-colonised discourses, and the participatory nature of K-fandom, high culture like Korean language and cultural customs have also increased their presence in Western regions. The K-Wave has been unique in this respect, with a notably semiotically productive fanbase, who subsequently need and desire the tools to participate in this respect. This involvement, particularly linguistically, contributes to the formation of a solidarity among members that is demonstrably powerful, hence granting K-fandom their notorious 'army' status. For instance, as well as ferociously championing their idols, K-fandom have even joined political debates, going as far as to organise protests. In one well-known case, they disrupted a Trump rally by purchasing most of the tickets and not turning up, leaving the rally without supporters.[13] K-fandoms have also joined in with public debates on issues such as Asian Hate and Black Lives Matter, following BTS's visit to the White House.[14]

## A bird's eye view of the K-Wave

If we look back to the early days of the K-Wave, Korea's increase in exports was originally driven by a desire to recuperate in the wake of the 1997 Asian Financial Crisis.[15] Korean cultural products gained popularity across Asia, before spreading to the West, in an endeavour enabled by the government's official national policy for the global reach of Korean cultural products known as '*Segyehwa*' (세계화).[16]

Yong divides the K-Wave into three phases which, although the focus of the discussion is often on K-film, is applicable across the various factions of the K-Wave: "Hallyu 1.0", which consists of "Hallyu 1.1" (1995–2000) and "Hallyu part 1.2" (2001–2006), and the "New Korean Wave era" (2007 onwards).[17] He also defines a period of accumulation before the K-Wave period as the "pre-Korean Wave era" (1989–1994). Yong defines Hallyu 1.0 primarily as an era of globalisation and hybridisation. The period was also important because domestic capital, such as that provided by large conglomerates, was withdrawn from the film market, resulting in financial difficulties for film production companies. Yong argues Hallyu 1.1 and 1.2 overlap in a continuation of the hybrid era, with Hollywood styles, skills, effects, and financial capital being adopted by domestic film producers, resulting in hybridisation. Hallyu 1.1 and 1.2 are distinguishable though, because independent producers became the major players after corporations like Samsung left the film production market in the latter. The influence of digital platforms was not significant during Hallyu 1.0 – smartphones were not introduced until 2007, and YouTube was not created until 2005. By the final year of Hallyu 1.2, K-film was the sixth leading film industry in the world.

Yong separates the New Korean Wave era, or 'Hallyu 2.0', from Hallyu 1.0 based on its distinctive differences in major characteristics. Primarily, these are the cultural forms that were exported in this period, and the technological developments, fandom, and cultural policies being implemented by the government. Hallyu 1.0 included primarily films, television dramas, technologies, and online games, with the main regions of their reach being within East Asia, and consumers typically in their 30s/40s. The government's cultural policies at that time were supportive but indirect. The New Korean Wave era, however, exported pop music, film, television dramas, animation, video, digital games, and technologies, including social media (smartphones, social networking service). The reach of these products extended beyond just Asia, to Europe, and to North America, with consumers increasingly becoming teenagers and those in their 20s. During this time, Yong argues that the government's cultural policies became more "direct" and "hands-on".[18]

The New Korean Wave era directly follows the implementation of a new cultural policy that changed the screen-quota system in the Korean film industry in 2006. By 2012, the Korean film industry had regained momentum and increased its market share and foreign exports further, and this development in foreign exports sets the period apart from the late 1990s and early 2000s. Since 2008, the export of cultural products, including broadcasting, movies, music, and games, surpassed the import of cultural products, with the overall import of foreign cultural goods declining. Korea achieved a surplus in cultural trade in 2008, and this continued until 2014. The popularity of local culture in the global market depends upon the border-crossing reach provided by digital technology and social media, because it is through this that popular culture can be accessed conveniently and with ease by diverse consumer demographics. Platforms such as YouTube, Instagram, Twitter, and Viki have been key in providing this access to Korean popular culture.

Although Yong names 1989–1994 as the 'pre-Wave era', it was an important step in the development of the K-Wave, and it also arguably started slightly earlier than 1989. The period, if one is to mark it out, began in 1986 when the Korean government first began to loosen its grip on creative industries. Take the film industry for example, which among the many factions of the K-Wave was one of those that went through a remarkable transformation. Film, which was the earliest and longest-standing leading faction of the K-Wave, closely followed by the K-drama, was finally opened to global film studios as restrictions on imports began to ease in 1986. Then, in 1988 these restrictions were removed entirely. Foreign film companies were even allowed to set up branch offices in Korea, and Korean films had to compete on equal terms with foreign films. Major Hollywood studios were the first to open branch offices in South Korea. First United International Pictures in March 1988, followed by Twentieth Century Fox in August 1988, Warner Bros. in 1989, Columbia Tristar in 1990, and Disney in 1993.

There have been popular culture waves before – the anime of Japan, the *telenovelas* of Mexico and Brazil, the Kung-Fu movies of 1970s and 1980s Hong Kong – however, the K-Wave is the only wave to export all its major cultural products simultaneously and to maintain popularity.[19] Arguably, this was possible because the K-Wave was able to benefit from the accessibility and participation enabled by social media, which other waves did not have, at least not at the same degree of development. Social media provided a platform for the K-fandom to communicate and participate constantly, removing the limitations imposed pre–social media by travel, time, and finance. Naturally, discourses were also able to hybridise further, and the snowball effect was able to hybridise in ways more dynamic than ever before, through which the K-Wave only grew in accessibility for consumers around the globe.

## The stats

The contribution of the K-Wave to the Korean economy has been significant. In 2004, popular culture constituted 0.2% of Korea's gross domestic product, which was approximately USD 1.87 billion. By 2019, it was estimated to have jumped to USD 12.3 billion.[20] This leap is perhaps unsurprising considering its success exporting all its major cultural products. For instance, when Spotify released its global K-Pop hub in 2021, it reported that the monthly average K-pop streams worldwide reached over 7.97 billion.

According to the Korea Foundation, which has conducted periodic surveys to keep track of the growth of K-fandom, there were 9.26 million K-fans in 2012 when the first survey was conducted of 85 countries. By 2019, the number had risen to 89 million in 113 countries, with over 70 million of the fans residing in Asia and Oceania, 11.8 million residing in the Americas, and 6.6 million residing in Europe. Then, in 2022, the Korea Foundation released a new report from a survey, this time conducted in cooperation with 152 countries, recording a total of 156.6 million fans as of December 2021.

Statista.com recently reported that according to a survey of 3,318 entertainment agencies, the total sales value of the Korean pop culture and arts industry increased to roughly 7.86 trillion South Korean won between 2014 and 2020, with the sales value of management agencies at 4.48 trillion South Korean won and production agencies at roughly 3.38 trillion won.[21]

If we look at just Netflix alone, Korea's domination of popular culture markets today is clearly visible. It was recently reported that K-dramas are leading Netflix's list of most-watched non-English shows.[22] If we consider the continuing growth of Netflix viewership globally, Korean culture and language have the potential to recalibrate societies in which Eurocentrism has been dominant. This year, Netflix's growth has been predicted to excel to 617.4 million viewers worldwide, which is 7.9% of the world's population. By 2024, that figure is predicted to reach 670.7 million (8.4%).[23] It was reported that on the week ending 27 February 2022, four out of 10 most-watched non-English-language releases on Netflix's Global Top 10 weekly were K-dramas.[24] Among them, it was the fifth week in a row that *Jigeum Uri Hakgyoneun* (지금 우리 학교는) '*All of Us Are Dead*' (2022) made the list with a total of 38,860,000 hours of viewership. In third place stood the newly released Netflix original *Sonyeon Simpan* (소년 심판) '*Juvenile Justice*', which had approximately 17,410,000 hours of viewing, following its debut on 25 February 2022.

This success is not surprising, however, as East Asia is leading Netflix's production markets in the volume of television shows and movies that they are producing. As Chin at NME explains, "Almost five percent of globally released Netflix Originals and Exclusives in 2019 were made in South Korea. Other Asian nations like India and China have only 2.1 and 1.9% shares respectively. [. . .] On the other end of the spectrum, the share of former key production markets has been declining over the last couple of years. Canada, for example, was responsible for roughly eight percent of the global output of exclusive Netflix content in 2017 before it fell behind South Korea in 2019 with a share of 4.3 percent." The push of international productions began as early as 2017, when only 34 of the 65 Netflix Originals in production at the time were made in the US.[25]

The popularity of K-content is also shown in the statistics that show why foreigners are engaging with Korea in other ways, such as travel. For instance, in another survey the share of tourists visiting Korea for K-pop and K-Wave experiences throughout 2021 (by age group) was investigated in a study involving 928 participants. People up to 59 years of age were found to visit for K-Wave experiences, with 12.2% of tourists aged between 15 and 19 years and 8.9% of people 20–29 years of age doing so.[26]

Statistics also show an increase in university students choosing to learn the Korean language. In the US, for instance, there was an overwhelming increase in Korean language learning, and other East Asian language learning, while there was a decrease in European language learning. Buchholz explains, "A hype around Korean pop music and pop culture has led to more students in the U.S. taking up Korean language classes, according to numbers released by the U.S. Modern Language Association. Between 2006 and 2016, the number of university students enrolled in Korean language classes almost doubled – the biggest increase for any language of 1,000 students or more.[27] Korean language provisions have responded by increasing their capacity for teaching globally. The number of King Sejong Institutes, for instance, totalled 213 worldwide in June 2020, established across 76 nations.[28] The acquisition of the Korean language – the K-Wave's influence on high- as well as low-culture acquisition (e.g., verbal language as well as popular culture) – indicates that *K-* has a new cultural potential and perhaps even the potential to be a model for 'glocal' communication.

Thus, unravelling the dimensions of *K-*, and getting to the hybridity at its heart, has never been timelier. Especially since Twitter saw 7.8 billion tweets globally about the K-Wave in 2021, with the previous record being 6.7 billion tweets in 2020. That is an astounding number of conversations happening globally about K-content and is particularly significant if we consider that the world's population in 2020 was only 7.753 billion,[29] with a rise to 8.0 billion estimated in 2022.[30]

## Why the K-Wave on-screen through words and objects?

There have been books that unravel the cultural discourses beyond the subtitle for foreign viewers of K-content on-screen, in response to growing interest among today's informed viewership for whom visibility matters.[31] However, this is the first book to focus on the elusive yet undeniable hybrid discourses in K-content. This unknown territory is key for understanding not only the K-Wave but also the hybrid societies we are living in today; as such, it is fundamental subject matter for scholars and consumers of the future. We endeavour to explore this K-ness through the verbal and visual footages provided by the multimodality 'on-screen', because it is the objects and words viewed on-screen that foreign viewers are recycling to create the unique snowball effect that characterises Hallyu 3.0. We collected a selection of objects and words, though not an exhaustive list by any means, from K-films, dramas, and even vlogs.

Each chapter is named after a core resource from which we have extracted objects and words, and within that chapter we also give a nod to other resources when applicable, though we use the lens of the primary resource for the main discussion. This simplifies matters for the reader who wishes to follow up on the original resources, which some researchers inevitably will. Chapters unfold through a combination of informative text and dialogue between the three authors. This method of presentation was devised to unfold the *K-* dynamically. *K-* is by no means traditional, and so it seems redundant to attempt to address it in a traditional way. Dialogue also provides subjectivity of opinions and personal experiences that are characteristic of Hallyu 3.0, but by experts in this field of research.

## Notes

1 Go to the V&A Museum website for more information on *Hallyu! The Korean Wave* exhibition: www.vam.ac.uk/articles/k-pop-fandom
2 The BBC's Recipe for Dalgona Coffee: www.bbcgoodfood.com/recipes/dalgona-coffee
3 Vegan Matcha Dalgona Coffee Recipe: https://vegarecepten.com/en/vegan-matcha-dalgona-latte/
4 Healthy Foody Ph's Matcha Dalgona Recipe: https://youtu.be/yB0xt66Is4Q
5 Dalgona Latte Recipe: www.youtube.com/watch?v=gqX10ED66AM
6 Strawberry Dalgona Recipe by *Simply Mamá Cooks* (1.48 million subscribers): www.youtube.com/watch?v=4_0aMn8I2Nc
7 Honeysuckle (1.17 million subscribers) Shared a variety of dalgona recipes (with 1,597,575 views): www.youtube.com/watch?v=Aaqc2jFcYO8
8 The Happy Noona Shared 'How to Make Dalgona Coffee/Frothy Coffee': www.youtube.com/watch?v=bqqANy2EoKI
9 McCurry, Justin. 2020. "How US K-Pop Fans Became a Political Force to Be Reckoned With." www.theguardian.com/music/2020/jun/24/how-us-k-pop-fans-became-a-political-force-to-be-reckoned-with-blm-donald-trump
10 Glück, Antje. 2018. "De-Westernization and Decolonization in Media Studies." In *Oxford Research Encyclopedia of Communication*. Oxford: Oxford University Press. https://doi.org/10.1093/acrefore/9780190228613.013.898
11 Kiaer, Jieun, and Loli Kim. 2021. *Understanding Korean Film; A Cross-Cultural Perspective*. London: Routledge.
12 There are many examples of articles written by K-film/drama viewers. One example worth a reading is: 'Subtitles Can't Capture the Full Class Critique in "Parasite"' by S. Cho (2020). https://gen.medium.com/subtitles-cant-capture-the-full-class-critique-in-parasite-27d36748db9d
13 Evelyn, Kenya. 2020. "Trump 'played' by K-Pop Fans and TikTok Users Who Disrupted Tulsa Rally." *The Guardian*. www.theguardian.com/us-news/2020/jun/21/trump-tulsa-rally-scheme-k-pop-fans-tiktok-users
14 BTS visit the White House to discuss Asian hate with President Biden: www.bbc.co.uk/news/world-us-canada-61649521

15 Chua, Beng Huat, and Koichi Iwabuchi, eds. 2008. *East Asian Pop Culture*. Hong Kong: Hong Kong University Press. https://doi.org/10.5790/hongkong/9789622098923.001. 0001

16 Lee, Sue Jin. 2011. "The Korean Wave: The Seoul of Asia." *The Elon Journal of Undergraduate Research in Communications*, 2(1), pp. 85–93.

17 Yong, Jin Dal. 2016. *New Korean Wave*. Chicago, IL: University of Illinois Press. https://doi.org/10.5406/illinois/9780252039973.001.0001

18 Yong, Jin Dal. 2016. *New Korean Wave*. Chicago, IL: University of Illinois Press. https://doi.org/10.5406/illinois/9780252039973.001.0001

19 Kim, Loli, and Jieun Kiaer. 2022. "A Theory of Multimodal Translation for Cross-Cultural Viewers of South Korean Film." PhD diss., Oxford: University of Oxford.

20 "Korean Wave (Hallyu) – The Rise of Korea's Cultural Economy & Pop Culture." *Martin Roll: Business & Brand Leadership*, 2021. https://martinroll.com/resources/articles/asia/korean-wave-hallyu-the-rise-of-koreas-cultural-economy-pop-culture/

21 To view Statista's report, go to: www.statista.com/statistics/932760/south-korea-pop-culture-arts-industry-total-sales-by-business-type/

22 "Korean Wave (Hallyu) – The Rise of Korea's Cultural Economy & Pop Culture." *Martin Roll: Business & Brand Leadership*, 2021. https://martinroll.com/resources/articles/asia/korean-wave-hallyu-the-rise-of-koreas-cultural-economy-pop-culture/

23 To view Statista's report, go to: www.statista.com/chart/25876/share-of-netflix-originals-and-exclusives-released-worldwide-by-country-of-origin/

24 Kats, Rimma. 2022. "Netflix Statistics: How Many Subscribers Does Netflix Have? Worldwide, US Member Count and Growth." *Insider Intelligence*. www.insiderintelligence.com/insights/netflix-subscribers/

25 Ju, H. 2020. "Korean TV Drama Viewership on Netflix: Transcultural Affection, Romance, and Identities." *Journal of International and Intercultural Communication*, 13(1), pp. 32–48. http://doi.org/10.1080/17513057.2019.1606269

26 To view Statista's Report, go to: www.statista.com/statistics/1134941/south-korea-tourists-visiting-for-hallyu-experiences-by-age-group/

27 To view Statista's Report, go to: www.statista.com/chart/19598/increase-in-students-enrolled-in-different-language-classes-at-us-universities/

28 To view Statista's Report, go to: www.statista.com/statistics/1124508/king-sejong-institute-number-of-institutes-by-continent/

29 Data Commons Place Explorer. 2022. "Earth." https://datacommons.org/place/Earth? utm_medium=explore&mprop=count&popt=Person&hl=en

30 Department of Economic and Social Affairs Population Division. 2022. *World Population Prospects 2022*. New York: Department of Economic and Social Affairs Population Division.

31 Kiaer, Jieun, and Loli Kim. 2021. "One-Inch-Tall Barrier of Subtitles: Translating Invisibility in Parasite." In Y. Kim (Ed.), *Soft Power of the Korean Wave:* Parasite, *BTS and Drama*. London: Routledge.

# 2

# *SQUID GAME*

For the past 3 years, the Korean Wave has reached an all-new peak in its success, as it has shifted into the mainstream, and *Ojingeo Geim* (오징어 게임) 'Squid Game' (2021) played a big part in that shift, alongside its predecessor *Parasite* (2019). We believe that this book should begin with *Squid Game* because of the impact that it has had on popular culture around the globe. The instant hit television series broke Netflix records in 2021, at one point reaching the number 1 spot on the Netflix charts in at least 90 different countries around the world.[1] The series won countless awards, many of which were ceremonies in the West that had been, until recently, elusive to those outside of Hollywood. Lee Jung-jae, who plays the protagonist Gi-hun, was the first Asian person to win an Emmy for Best Male Actor in a Drama (2022).[2] Lee Yoo-mi who plays Na-yeon also won an Emmy for Best Guest Actress in a Drama (2022); and Oh Yeong-su who plays Oh Il-nam won the Golden Globe Award for Best Supporting Actor in a Series, Miniseries, or Motion Picture Made for Television (2022).[3] Indeed, *Squid Game* encompasses everything that *K-* is.

The series provides an extremified glimpse into the disparity between classes in Korea – issues local to Koreans, but also that can be relatable globally. Gi-hun is a failure in all respects. He is divorced, a prolific gambler, in serious debt, and neglecting his duties as a father and son. When loan-sharks begin to demand Gi-hun's organs as repayment, his life hits an all-time rock-bottom. As if by magic, he is invited to play a mysterious game for a chance to win a cash prize. Little does he know the game has fatal consequences for those who lose.

In this chapter, we bring some of the key objects and excerpts of dialogue from *Squid Game* to the discussion table, using them as lenses through which it is possible to unfold the various dimensions of *K-*. But, before we talk about objects, let's present a few thoughts on *Squid Game* and its K-ness. The success of *Squid Game* raises questions about the nature of *K-*, such as, "where is Korean-ness or K-ness

DOI: 10.4324/9781003203230-2

in the show?' Traditional high culture isn't really a focal point in *Squid Game*. Instead, the culture reflected is very different from what Korean people think of when they think about Korean (traditional) culture. Koreans are very happy that the show has received praise and awards, but they do not think of it as representative of Korean culture. This shows both that K-content is a transcultural entity – less about Korean-ness and more about universalism as depicted in Korean culture – and confirms that *Squid Game* is a part of this K-content. Squid Game's universal components include survival, desperation, and urban hardship, which appeals to many, and has especially been at the forefront in recent times since COVID-19.

### Training suit

*Loli:* We begin our discussion with the use of shape and colour in the costumes and sets of *Squid Game*. The visual is striking as it is original, which seemed to attract viewers as much as the narrative. This could be seen early on after the release of the show in the production and wearing of the costumes and masks by fans. The story itself – the idea of rich people paying for the pleasure of others being killed – is not new, nor is it unique to Korea alone. One of the most well-known examples of this is the *Hostel* film franchise (2005, 2007, 2011), and the concept appears in micro-forms in a variety of films and dramas. *Squid Game* is then made original by its unique presentation of the concept – the infusion of the narrative with Korean culture, and at the same time K-culture. The aesthetic plays an important role in this. From the umbrella, triangle, and circle symbols to the pink jumpsuits worn by the guards, and the turquoise training suits worn by contestants – this is branding, using complex and practical cultural forms. Can you tell us a little about these colours and shapes, their meanings, and contexts?

FIGURE 2.1 Contestants wearing the training suit, in *Squid Game*.

*Jieun:* First, the uniform – '*teuraining* suit' as we call them in Korean – shows that the contestants are in 'game mode'. When playing games, Koreans like to wear uniforms to define the 'game space', and also to signify their teams. On Korean primary school playgrounds, the colours used to do so are typically red and blue. *Squid Game* gives this intertext a little twist, emphasising that although a game, this is by no means an orthodox situation, by using brighter more unusual shades of these colours, opting for bright pink and dark turquoise. Also, the uniforms are one of the many ways that the show plays with irony. It is a strategy used to twist things – to be duplicitous – and convey the psychological nature of the game in the aesthetic as well as narrative. The uniforms not only signify game mode for Koreans, but something along the lines of 'This is not a serious situation – it's just a game!' They create a false sense of relaxedness for both the players within the game and those viewing. While, in fact, the situation couldn't be less serious, since contestants are gambling with their lives, and the odds are not in their favour.

*Loli:* Most importantly here is 'how' aesthetic elements are played with ironically because it is Korean cultural intertexts that are used to create the irony, and yet they still achieve what they set out to do among both Korean and non-Korean audiences.

*Jieun:* Exactly! Another irony in the uniform, which links to the concept of being in game mode, but also translates well into Western contexts, is how the contestants wear the same uniform as if they are on the same team, and yet they are competing against each other. This again creates a false sense of reality, in which there is solidarity temporarily or superficially – a false sense of safety, and in some cases of friendship – with the contestants eventually having or choosing to betray and ultimately kill each other. Gi-hun's childhood friendship with fellow contestant Sang-woo, the seemingly budding friendship between Sang-woo and Ali Abdul, the short-lived alliance between Deok-su and Mi-nyeo, or the husband and wife who entered the competition together – in all of these relationships, they are forced to make a choice to live or die or to kill or save. In one case, a husband and wife who entered the game together had to choose which one of them would die. If they do not, the guards will kill them anyway.

*Loli:* Other objects to convey irony include the scoreboard. It calculates the number of people eliminated, and the cash prize as it increases after each game. The irony here uses a similar strategy as the uniforms: it makes light of the deaths, as if they have been eliminated from the game but not killed, though by this point all the contestants have played the game and know that the number is of deaths and not losers.

Another example of irony created aesthetically is in the design of the contestants' coffins. The boxes are made to look like gift boxes, with elaborate bows. Again, there is a misalignment of symbols with situations here.

The scoreboard, like the uniforms, holds Korean cultural intertexts that create irony; however, this is also a universal context that creates this irony too. Do you think the colours of the uniforms are aspects of the K-ness we have been discussing in the previous chapter?

*Jieun:* I don't think the colours or even the shapes are *K-* itself, but rather *K-* is a range of multimedia, and under the umbrella of each media element are multimodal imprints. Viewers are left with shapes and colours, and even sounds, which form subsets of *K-* that remain as footage in the memories of viewers. These are extremely small fragments of the *K-*, which are incredibly difficult to define in terms of *K-*, as *K-* itself is constantly in flux and incredibly dynamic.

*Loli:* In this respect, *K-* is very much like the Korean language.

*Jieun:* Only, unlike the Korean language, which has a standard structure and vocabulary, *K-* doesn't have clear or fixed definitions. We can sit here and discuss it, and recognise its existence, and at the same time find it difficult to say emphatically that this or that 'is *K-*'. Therefore, when it comes to *Squid Game*, although we can never say that the colours or shapes used are certainly *K-*, we can say that they are elements of *Squid Game* as a part of *K-*.

*Loli:* We then see those shapes, colours – the various elements of visual footage – transmitted beyond the screen. That's where in Hallyu 3.0, the snowball effect was able to gain such incredible momentum. In addition to being able to buy replicas of the costumes like the training suits from *Squid Game*, we see actual tracksuits for sale with signifiers of *Squid Game*, such as the shapes from the logo, being sold online. It is almost an evolution – the idea of a training suit in the real world – which for Westerners is a tracksuit that one wears without necessarily being on a team or playing a game – and then marking that with symbols that are unmistakably from *Squid Game*.

## Mask

*Loli:* Then we have the masks worn by the guards in the game, which universally viewers will interpret to hide their identities. But the shapes on the masks signify the hierarchy between them – something that we find out as the episodes in the series progress.

*Jieun:* Yes, there is a hierarchy, signified using shapes, and then the main boss has an entirely different mask, which nobody else has, making it clear that he has an important position. Likewise, the senior boss, whose existence the viewer is not made aware of until late in the series, also has a mask. However, his mask, like the wealthy gamblers who visit the Island where the game is held to watch the final games, is of an animal, and ornate and flamboyant.

*Loli:* The use of shapes to signify rank, opposed to say colour, or stripes on their shirt, for instance, is perhaps a part of branding the show – the shapes especially fit in well with the concept of games, and always remind me of game

**FIGURE 2.2**  The guards wearing their hierarchical masks, in *Squid Game*.

controllers, which have a triangle, circle, square, cross button. At the same time, they fit in well with the shapes in the famous '*dalgona* challenge'. There are different associations and subsequently ways of relating to these aesthetic choices.

These aspects have assimilated into *K-* extremely well. One example that I found to be particularly demonstrative is Christmas cookie cutters made in the shape of people wearing Christmas hats (Santa or reindeer) and the masks from *Squid Game*; one with a triangle shape, another with a circle, and another with a square on the front of its mask.

*Jieun:*  For Koreans, the hierarchy is relatable on another level too, because Korean society is fundamentally hierarchical. In families, between work colleagues, even in friendships hierarchy must be accounted for unless those involved are the same age.

*Loli:*  Since the guards hardly ever interact, it makes sense to make their hierarchy be visually coded. I imagine this felt more natural than simply making everyone equal, as this would be quite difficult given that simply being born in the year after someone then means that you must respect them. It is therefore the logical choice for Koreans to introduce a means of communicating the existing hierarchy, which in this case is the shapes, and styles.

In the show, when we find out that the soldiers' hierarchy can be inferred based on the shapes on their masks, another character – an undercover policeman who has snuck onto the island in search of his missing brother – is simultaneously discovering this. By wearing a soldier's uniform while trying to blend in, he begins to realise that the shapes signify rank, and subsequently where they can go, and what they should be doing at certain times; and how breaking the rules can result in being disciplined by a senior.

*Jieun:*  Also, although the contestants don't wear masks, they have a hierarchy too, and it is also difficult to translate, and therefore can only be interpreted through *K-*. The contestants look equal; however, for them there is inequality due to gender, age, and nationality (Korean or immigrant). Despite all the contestants being at rock-bottom in their lives, they still have this hierarchy and must navigate it.

*Loli:* It would be interesting to discover how many non-Koreans who are purchasing products like the cookie cutters are aware of the hierarchy signified by the shapes, and further how meaningful this is for Koreans.

## Korean neighbourhood

*Loli:* Landscape plays an important role in episode 6. The marbles game is played in a set built to look like a real Korean neighbourhood, and Gi-hun feels as though he recognises it, while Il-nam behaves as if this was his neighbourhood once. The small houses on the set are not common in Seoul. In fact, in the city, practically everybody lives in apartments. Houses are found outside of the capital city and are more popular in the countryside, and subsequently this design serves to signify certain associations. Whereas for non-Koreans it is almost maze-like and signifies little about Korean society. One can perhaps imagine it is a suburb somewhere, and perhaps it is linked to the narrative. What do you think those are? Does it feel purposeful?

*Jieun:* I can't say how this will be significant in the narrative of *Squid Game*. Perhaps we shall find that out in Season 2 when it's released. I can say, though, that this set shows a representation of the forgotten Seoul. It is the Seoul we see in another popular K-drama *Eungdaphara 1988* (응답하라 1988) 'Reply 1988' (2015–2016). This is a neighbourhood like those before Seoul underwent rapid modernisation. Seoul was overcrowded at that time, and hence the need to build up – removing houses and replacing them with apartment blocks that we see dominating the Seoul landscape today.

*Loli:* This landscape is taken from a time when neighbourhoods in Seoul were tight-knit. Neighbours were in each other's houses and in each other's business! There is a wonderful scene in *Reply 1988*, in which parents send their children from house to house to give the side dishes they've made to their neighbours at dinner time, and their neighbours do the same in return, until they each have a variety of side dishes on the table ready for dinner. It was a way of managing in hard times, and the crowded housing areas facilitated practices like these, and I imagine today are nostalgically looked upon with these memories by those who lived in them at the time.

## Dalgona

*Dalgona* is featured in episode 3 of *Squid Game*. This snack food is also a sort of game in Korea because the biscuit has a shape carved in the centre, and if you manage to cut it out with a needle without breaking it, then you win another for free.

That's why the contestants who chose an umbrella are upset, because they know how difficult it is to cut these shapes out, whereas the triangle and circle are much easier.

*Loli:*    It is probably a good time to mention that it isn't actually called *dalgona* in Korea, it's called *popgi*.

*Jieun:*  Nobody knows where the word *dalgona* came from. Like many things *K-*, the origin isn't traditional Korean culture or language, but 'something else', at least in its non-Korean contexts. *Popgi* involves another set of meanings, associations, and nostalgia for Koreans, though *popgi* has even undergone rejuvenation in Korea because of *Squid Game*.

**FIGURE 2.3**   The *dalgona* sugar biscuit as it is featured in the *dalgona* game featured in *Squid Game*.

**FIGURE 2.4**   Children running over to the *popgi* seller at the playground, in *Squid Game*.

*Popgi* was not ever considered particularly special in Korea. It is considered as low culture – the kind of thing your mother would deter you from buying on the way home from school. You would often find *popgi* stalls at the rear gate of the school. As I would leave for school in the morning, my own mother would yell to me "don't get *popgi* after school!" Good children wouldn't buy it as their parents wouldn't approve. It was through *Squid Game*, however, that *popgi* was revived and reborn as *dalgona* in both Korea and around the world, with a completely different – trendy, cool, transnational – perception attached to it.

*Loli:*   *K-* is so dynamic that cultural concepts can be reconfigured and relabelled for transnational interpretation and use. The key ingredient is hybridity.

FIGURE 2.5   Both the terms '*dalgona*' and '*popgi*' are now used in Korea, where they weren't before, such as on this sign at an establishment where children can make their own *popgi*.

*Jieun:* K-objects like *popgi* are picked up quite arbitrarily in this process. *Kimbap* (김밥) likewise has become very popular through *K*-content. Like *popgi*, Kimbap is not considered a sophisticated national dish by Koreans but rather an inexpensive, easy-to-make snack food. Simply wrap rice, vegetables, and potentially fish or meat, in a sheet of dried seaweed (*gim*, 김), and there you have it! It is like making a sandwich in the West. This is similar for the case of *ramyeon* instant noodles, which entered popular culture following the release of *Parasite* (2019), and like *popgi* was also renamed *'ramdon'* and was revived and reborn in its K-form as such. In this case, though, we know where this name came from, as it was developed by *Parasite's* (2019) subtitler Darcy Paquet, who invented the term.[4]

You will perhaps notice that *popgi, kimbap*, and *ramyeon* all have something in common – they are easy to make, with their ingredients widely available, and inexpensive to buy/make. K-foods have increased in popularity because they have been seen in films and dramas and other forms of visual K-content, and viewers then want to try it; but the foods that are picked up align with the participatory nature of fandom today, as well as their desire to create solidarity online. Traditional Korean foods, that is to say those that are considered more sophisticated in Korea, are much more complex to make, and not simple for everyone to make and share. Therefore, it's more difficult for these foods to become popular culture, as we saw with the *dalgona* craze, which not only was popularised, but it also evolved into further trends like *dalgona* coffee.

Platforms such as TikTok, and Roblox where people can make and share games, are places where popular culture crazes like those of *Squid Game* have been able to thrive – from the games themselves, to challenges and shared experiences of the foods picked up from the show. Red Light, Green Light (2021)[5] is one such Roblox game.

*Loli:* Anyone can take part, so the 'informed consumers' of today – who want to participate – can do so without jumping through hoops. It isn't stepping into the unknown. Simply go down to the local supermarket and prepare at home. This also facilitates a unique multimodal engagement with K-content, and a subsequent interpretation of *K-*, that 'snowballs' reinstating and developing *K-*.

### Ddakji

*Ddakji* (딱지) is another example of K-content that is accessible and inexpensive to pick up. The goal of the game is to flip over your opponent's *ddakji* piece by throwing your *ddakji* on it. If you manage to turn your opponent's *ddakji* over, then you can take it. Some people have compared *ddakji* to the American game Pogs, which was popular during the 1990s; however, there are slight differences in the pieces used in either game.

There are many *jeontongnori* (전통놀이), Korean 'traditional games'. *Squid Game* uses some of these, specifically those played by children.[6] Some of the games are played outside of Korea too, such as 'marbles' and 'tug of war'. There are several ancient variations of tug of war across Asia, which have been around for thousands of years. In ancient Korea, the game was known as *juldarigi* (줄다리기) and was often played at festivals, such as the lunar festival. In fact, it still is today, with it believed that the winning village receives a bountiful harvest that year.

Several games are local to Korea, and among them is *ddakji*, which is perhaps one of the easier games for viewers to try. Making the folded paper tiles – the *ddakji* pieces – is simple. They are traditionally made by folding paper, and even young children can master this without the help of an adult.

## Hibiscus flower

The hibiscus – or as it is called in Korea, *mugunghwa* (무궁화) – is the national flower of South Korea and has been a symbol of the region since ancient times, adopted as a symbol of the Joseon dynasty (1392–1910), and similarly by the Silla Kingdom (57 BC–935 AD), which named itself '*Mugunghwa* Country'. *Mugunghwa* is also the namesake of *Mugunghwa Kkochi Piotsseumnida* (무궁화 꽃 이 피었 습니다) 'the hibiscus flower is blooming' that is featured in *Squid Game* – a playground game in Korea that viewers have been re-enacting around the world.

*Jieun:* People from around the world have been playing the game, which before *Squid Game*, non-Koreans hadn't really heard of. It is a children's game, but *Squid Game* made it popular among an entirely different age group who are interested in the game for different reasons than Korean children. There are some similarities to the game Red Light, Green Light, which is popular in Western regions, and it is even referred to as this in the English subtitles; however, even Red Light, Green Light was not popular among adults before.

*Loli:* Also, the game is more different from Red Light, Green Light than people think. The interaction between non-Koreans and the game is a little different conceptually in this respect. The clue is in the name of the game – *Mugunghwa Kkochi Piotsseumnida*. Red Light, Green Light involves one player having their back to the wall while others try to cross the finish line. A player is eliminated if they get caught moving during a red light. The red or green light allows players to move or warns them to stop moving, and so the decision for when players can run and must stop is not solely at the discretion of the person calling the colours. However, *Mugunghwa Kkochi Piotsseumnida*, which translates as 'the hibiscus flower is blooming', has no red or green light. Instead, *Mugunghwa Kkochi Piotsseumnida* relies

FIGURE 2.6   The child robot who infamously plays *Mugunghwa Kkochi Piotsseumnida* with the contestants in *Squid Game*.

upon orderly cadence. When the contestants in *Squid Game* play *Mugunghwa Kkochi Piotsseumnida*, we see this in how the players are allowed to move when the motion sensor robot recites "*mugunghwa kkochi piotsseumnida*", and when the sentence ends the girl turns and anyone caught moving is eliminated. The phrase doesn't change either, so players know when to run and when to stop. The only thing that can be changed is the tempo of the phrase, which when spoken more quickly increases the difficulty.

## Loan-shark's contract

*Loli:*   Early in the first episode of *Squid Game*, we are presented with a series of events that set the scene of the protagonist (Gi-hun) and his problematic life. In one scene, after seeing Gi-hun steal money from his mother for gambling, he is assaulted by thugs to whom he owes money, which again was spent gambling. The leader of the group forces him to sign a contract stating that if he does not pay the money back in the allotted time, he will provide his kidneys to pay off the debt.

Despite its extreme nature, this narrative is not uncommon. Further glimpses into the illegal organ selling industry can be seen later in *Squid Game*, when eliminated contestants' organs are harvested. Similar depictions can also be found in several popular K-blockbusters, for instance, Lee Jeong-beom's *Ajeossi* (아저씨) 'The Man From Nowhere' (2010), Kim Hong-seon's *Gongmojadeul* (공모자들) 'Traffickers' (2012), and Park Chan-wook's *Boksuneun Naui Geot* (복수는 나의 것) 'Sympathy for Mr Vengeance' (2002).

*Jieun:* Although less common than they were until the early millennium, these issues still exist in Korea. The rough and invasive practices of loan-sharks in Korea are well known (e.g., high interest rates, harassment, and violence), as is the illegal organ trafficking industry which subsequently enables practices like pledging organs to loan-sharks.[7]

According to the Consumer Loan Finance Association, the number of people borrowing from illegal private loan-sharks rose from 330,000 in 2015 to 430,000 in 2016. The amount of such loans doubled from an estimated 10.59 trillion won in 2015 to 24.11 trillion won in 2016. The amount borrowed on average rose from 32.1 million won in 2015 to 56.1 million won in 2016.[8]

*Loli:* I also have read claims by Koreans that they have pledged their organs before. The most notable case was the claim by the founder of biopharmaceutical company Celltrion, Seo Jung-jin, who is the second-richest person in South Korea after Samsung Electronics Co.'s chairman. He claims to have pledged his organs to get the funds to save his company after the Asian financial crisis in the early 2000s.[9]

Korean dramas like *Naui Ajeossi* (나의 아저씨) 'My Mister' (2018) provide a glimpse into the dangers of owing money to loan-sharks in Korea. Protagonist Ji-an works tirelessly only to hand the money over to debt collectors, after inheriting a debt from her mother. She is harassed at her home and at her workplace, with the debt collectors breaking and entering her home, threatening her and her family, beating her up, and even following and harassing the colleagues and friends who try to help her. She steals the leftovers from the plates that she is employed to wash at a restaurant in the evening because she can't afford food.

Issues relating to loan-sharks have become especially prominent of late, since the devastation caused to businesses during COVID-19. According to the *Los Angeles Times*, South Korea's household debt increased significantly in the second quarter of 2021, increasing more than 10% compared to the same period in the previous year.[10] Citizens in their 30s are the most severely affected, according to the Bank of Korea, having borrowed more than 260% of their income on average.[11] Disenchanted by employment possibilities, and with real estate prices rising, young adults have been increasingly investing in stocks or cryptocurrencies. Furthermore, government regulators reported roughly 300,000 illegal lending advertisements in 2020, which was a 30% increase from the year before.

Currently, unregistered money lenders are allowed to charge interest on private loans up to the statutory limit of 24% per annum like their legal peers, although it has been reported that illegal loans are charged as much as 311.3% interest. Moreover, due to lenders often having unacceptable credit ratings, there are additional conditions upon taking out these loans. Loan-sharks' debt-collecting processes differ by the type of interest rate charged (e.g., daily or monthly), the amount borrowed, and the purpose of the loan. However, conditions upon how and by when the debt must be paid are strict (including interest), and if not adhered to the lender is liable for harassment. This brings us to another commonly reported condition, which is that the lender must provide the names and contact details of ten family members and colleagues; should the lender not pay on time or in the correct manner, then they will visit them. The lender must also provide their home and work contact details. Finally, it has been reported that lenders are forced to answer their phones any time to the loan-shark, except for working hours.

*Loli:*  How was this situation able to develop?

*Jieun:*  It is the darker side of economic growth. It all began with Korea's industrialisation 60 years ago. People tend to talk only about the positive side of South Korea's dramatic economic transformation, and those left behind are forgotten. But this is a side effect of our success – we got here by being extremely competitive, and not everyone has the skills or social background to do so, and those who don't have at times been discarded. There were many casualties in the early days of industrialisation for instance, whose skills were no longer needed. The lives of people in the agricultural industry, for instance, were damaged beyond repair. The Korean classic *Sampoganeun Gil* (삼포가는 길) 'The Road to Sampo' (1975) depicts this tragic side of industrialisation. Many wandering labourers were produced as a result, and these people were deprived of their identities and their hometowns.[12] The same thing happens today, but at a microscale, for instance, when a company bankrupts and must let go of employees.

*Loli:*  All four characters, including Gi-hun, seem to find themselves in a similar sort of social purgatory, despite being set in different periods and circumstances.

*Jieun:*  Yes, it is a very real and feared situation in Korea. Particularly, for middle-aged people, and not only labourers but office workers, people who have devoted their lives to one company. Behind the glamorous image often painted of modern Korea, especially the capital city Seoul, are the millions of regular Koreans who struggle to power this machine. On average, Korean employees work 323 hours more than Japanese workers annually. Japanese employees are known for working themselves to death, which says a lot about the situation in Korea.

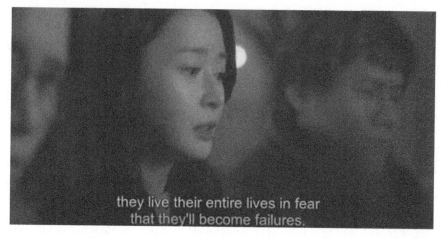

they live their entire lives in fear
that they'll become failures.

FIGURE 2.7   Friends discuss the difficulties of working for Korean companies, in *My Mister*.

*Loli:*   K-drama *My Mister* is another series that provides insight into this issue in the stories of regular people who work hard but are faced with the fear of being discarded by companies or organisations to whom they have pledged their loyalty; some finding themselves without work and turning to industries such as cleaning, as they have no other skills apart from those used in their previous role.

*Jieun:*   The severity of the social and psychological impact that this has on these people, as you can imagine, is significant. Financially, this often results in debt. It isn't easy to get hired by another company in Korea when you are late in your career, and usually you must work your way up. Also, the way professional communities encompass one's life in Korea, means that losing one's job feels more like expulsion from a community. It is more than simply changing where one works, and therefore involves a loss of identity. Colleagues and one's professional organisation are, for most Koreans, as much a part of their lives as their own families; in fact, many spend more time with their colleagues than their own family. In Korea, eating one's evening meal with colleagues instead of one's wife and children is not uncommon, and often difficult to avoid. The issue of displacement is therefore as much of an issue today as it was in the era depicted in *The Road to Sampo* (1975), and it arises from quite similar circumstances.

*Loli:*   How can people identify displacement in K-content?

*Jieun:*   Aside from the narrative, the displacement of the characters can be seen in their language. It often lacks etiquette, and yet this is not quarrelled over, which it would be under normal circumstances in Korea. This is unorthodox, and it reflects an unusual situation, in which the people feel they have nothing to lose and nothing to offer. They often neutralise or equalise language, removing etiquette that is considered mandatory. In the case of *The Road to Sampo* (1975), Young-dal and Mr Jeong have a mutual unspoken agreement to interact on these terms. They meet first, and despite the Korean cultural need to ask the age of a person to whom one is speaking to determine how to speak to them, the two men choose not to do so. Instead, they speak formally and politely throughout, and no attempt is made by either at any point to renegotiate this. They even avoid calling each other by name or address term, after using *noh-hyeong* (노형) 'old brother' on their first encounter, because in Korea address terms are used instead of names and which one you choose inevitably expresses hierarchy of intimacy. It would be normal to do so as their relationship develops, and especially since they are spending considerable time together. Mr Jeong, as the elder, would need to take on the senior role as Young-dal's *seonbae*, and this would involve the responsibility of 'taking care' of Young-dal. Due to Mr Jeong's desperate situation and uncertain future, he can't perform the role. At the same time, Young-dal can't be an attentive and obedient junior to Mr Jeong, as he needs to take care of himself while they travel in harsh conditions.

Loli:  Another method of avoiding mutual responsibility in a Korean relationship, at least in the sense of the care and obedience that we see between seniors and juniors, though it would normally reflect intimacy, is to speak as if they're equals with a close relationship with the agreement of both parties. We see this between Young-dal and Baek-hwa.

Jieun:  Yes, between Young-dal and Mr Jeong, the nature of their desperate situation means that they are not able to demand respect, nor do they wish to give it. However, because the age gap between them is less significant than between them and Mr Jeong, Young-dal and Baek-hwa make no effort at all to be polite, rather than remain formal throughout. Their communication is careless but intimacy-building. They are breaking social norms, reflecting both their desperation and the disconnection from their own identities. For instance, it would be totally unacceptable for a young woman like Baek-hwa to speak to a man who is a stranger so informally. She uses *banmal*, an informal style of speech reserved for intimates or for speaking to subordinates, when speaking to Young-dal. Her non-verbal expressions are just as informal and inappropriate. She frequently invades his space, patting him, and making eye contact with him. This is highly unorthodox. Baek-hwa is more polite to Mr Jeong, due to his age, but initially she uses *banmal* to him too, which he also tolerates.

Loli:  What similarities or connections do you see between the characters in *The Road to Sampo* and *Squid Game?*

Jieun:  Gi-hun, for instance, is a laid-off union autoworker, whose life fell into disarray after the company he worked for went bankrupt. In one scene, he remembers the violence that ensued when his co-workers attempted to protest the matter.

Gi-hun's back story was inspired by real events, in which Korean company SsangYong Motors laid off hundreds of autoworkers due to the company's bankruptcy in 2009. The employees then held a protest in the factory, demanding the return of their jobs. They were violently attacked by the police, who assaulted them with batons and water cannons, and dropped tear gas on them.[13]

*Loli:* We see a similar attitude expressed in the etiquette of Gi-hun too – linguistically, non-verbally, and in how he communicates his values in his actions.

*Jieun:* First, he expresses an absence of filial piety when he is with his mother at home. His expressions linguistically and non-verbally are less important here, as he is alone with his mother, so he can behave informally. However, he communicates his values (or lack of) by stealing from her, watching her struggle, and being self-serving and deceitful. Even when he gives his mother money, he gives less than he stole from her.

### Side dishes

*Loli:* There are also some smaller touches that I picked up on. Gi-hun has bad table manners, and it isn't just informal behaviour. In one scene, Gi-hun eats his dinner with his mother. On the table are two small bowls of rice, a plate of mackerel, and a selection of containers each filled with a different side dish. One of the side dishes is *baek kimchi* ('white kimchi'), which is a pickled cabbage without *gochu garu* ('red pepper powder'). In this scene, Gi-hun uses his spoon to take the *baek kimchi* from its container and eats it directly over the container. Korean side dishes are kept in the fridge for some time since many of them are fermented. While Koreans do, on occasion, eat side dishes directly from containers among intimates, it is polite to use chopsticks when they do, although generally they prefer to place small portions of side dishes into small serving dishes for hygiene. It is also not polite to eat directly over side dish containers, rather than one's own bowl, for the same reason. It's a small touch, but worth mentioning because interpretations culturally can vary, and all these behaviours serve to characterise him.

*Jieun:* Consuming side dishes like *baek kimchi*, which can have considerable juice in them, can be quite off-putting to others who are present. These are quite basic table manners, and so in general, it seems to be a way of aligning Gi-hun's attributes to present him as a character whose life has fallen into disarray.

*Loli:* Gi-hun's lack of Confucian values and etiquette are not only visible at home, so that's how we know there is more to these expressions than simply intimacy. He also displays unwillingness to conform to common courtesy when he interacts with strangers too.

**FIGURE 2.8**   Gi-hun playing *ddakji* with the stranger, in *Squid Game*.

*Jieun:* Yes, in the fateful scene when Gi-hun is invited to contend in the game, we see this in Gi-hun's attitude towards a smartly dressed stranger of clearly higher socio-economic status than Gi-hun – a situation that warrants a basic level of politeness. However, when the man speaks to Gi-hun, he speaks using a formal and polite speech style, *hapsyoche*, and is consistent in using polite deferential non-verbal gestures. He clasps his hands in his lap, leans forward at times, and averts his eye gaze. Gi-hun, however, speaks using the informal speech style *banmal*, and uses non-verbal gestures carelessly. He makes direct eye contact for lengthy periods, while speaking in *banmal*, just like Baek-hwa in *The Road to Sampo*.

In this case, though, the difference in social status of Gi-hun and the unknown man is more severe, and they are not so desperate as to treat etiquette as a trivial matter. Therefore, Gi-hun's choices in how he communicates are not empathetic, nor mutually agreed, as it was in *The Road to Sampo*. Though, while the social dynamic and the linguistic negotiation between the two men is different, the reason for Gi-hun behaving this way is the same – he is displaced and feels a loss of identity. Consequently, he is no longer operating within the bounds of acceptable cultural behaviour.

## Spoon

Our next object is metaphorical rather than physical, though nonetheless it is an important object: the spoon. We are not looking at actual spoons on the dinner table in *Squid Game* (2021), however, but the metaphorical spoons used to define social status in Korea, which are represented in one's qualifications, etiquette, clothing, and beyond. These spoons are carried with Koreans like invisible labels that tell other Koreans their social status. Officially the class system of the Joseon dynasty was abolished; however, unofficially the classes are still very clearly defined. *Spoon Class Theory* provides the needed definition. Synonymous with modern

Korean society, it speaks of a hereditary class system existing in Korea, creating a hopeless disparity and prolificating what is well known to Korean young professionals as 'hell *Joseon*'.

The class of Korean children is classified by spoons: gold spoons, silver spoons, copper spoons, plastic spoons, and clay spoons. The type of spoon is determined by the class of a child at birth.[14] The Golden Spoon family has assets of at least 2 billion won and an annual income of over 200 million won. In pounds, this currently is the equivalent to around £1,281,851.00, and an annual income of over £128,185.00. Slightly lower in the system are the Silver Spoon families, with assets of 1 billion won and an annual income of at least 80 million won. Silver Spoon families make up 3% of the total households in Korea. The offspring of Silver Spoon families occupy a place in Korean society's upper class, even if they are not as affluent as the Golden Spoon families. Then there are the Copper Spoon families, who have assets of 500 million won and an annual income of 55 million won. These make up 10% of families in Korea. These families can afford to pay high tuition fees, educating their children by the elite from their early years, and with a chance at getting into the top ten universities in Korea. Most ordinary Korean families are Plastic Spoon families, accounting for 80% of Korea's families. At the bottom of the system are the Clay Spoon families, who have no stable income, and even providing basic things for their children, such as food, is a problem.[15] Spoon Class Theory has even emerged in popular culture in recent years, often referred to as Gold Spoons and Dirt Spoons. Perhaps many will have seen the band BTS called a 'dirt spoon idol', due to their early struggles. Their song *Fire* (2016) even contains the lyrics, "Don't call me a spoon! I am just a human". There is also a popular fantasy webtoon (2016) turned television series (2022) called *Golden Spoon*, which features a poor boy swapping his family for his wealthy friend's family by eating with a magic gold spoon. Gold spoons themselves have, in fact, become a popular gift on children's first birthdays, replacing the gold rings that Koreans have traditionally given.

Gold Spoon families are often *chaebol* families, who under the *samgang oryun* (삼강오륜) 'The Three Bonds and Five Virtues' ideology, have managed to reinstate themselves as an alternative *yangban* (양반) 'noble' class, who behave as an autonomous dynasty. Even the conversational patterns, behaviour, and customs of *chaebol* and the service people around them are reminiscent of the Joseon nobility. For instance, when a *chaebol* CEO gives over his position to his son, the process is called *Seunggye* (승계). This is a word often used to refer to the succession of the kingship.

*Loli:*   Depictions of *chaebol* families can be seen in films such as *Hanyeo* (하녀) 'The Housemaid' (2010), *Beterang* (베테랑) 'Veteran' (2015), and even *Gisaengchung* (기생충) 'Parasite' (2019); though in *Parasite* and *The Housemaid* we do not encounter the extended family's organisation. The on-screen stories of these families often depict two primary things – the first is their social status overpowering all other hierarchies, including age, and the second is the difficulties that arise as a result.

*Jieun:* A common difficulty, which is depicted in *Gisaengchung*, is the loss of rank by those who hold equal or higher seniority in another ranking but are over-powered by the wealth of *chaebol* members. Another common issue is the mistreatment and advantage taken of juniors. This can be seen as a reflection of the sentiment of Koreans, who have expressed discontent regarding the power of the *chaebol*. This unrest over the insurmountable gap between rich and poor in Korea is fundamental in the narrative, and even the aesthetic. Ultimately, there is a cruelty in the furnishings of the game, a sarcasm that is very much directed at the players. This gap is incredibly important. It is the cause of unrest and repeated scandals in Korea. We call it *gapjil* (갑질), a term that refers to a situation in which a person with more power is abusing or overusing it.

*The New York Times* recently defined *gapjil* as "the abuse of underlings and sub-contractors by executives who behave like feudal lords".[16] Interestingly, the term *yangban*, to describe the ruling class, literally means "double order" in which the upper class can behave in ways that the lower class cannot, so the *chaebol* behaving like *yangban* is an idea that the term encapsulates.

Extreme cases of *gapjil* have been heavily covered by the media. One recent example was the "nut rage" incident in 2014. The daughter of a high-ranking airline official apparently forced an airline attendant to her knees and made the pilot turn the plane around, drop the attendant off, and then resume the flight all because the attendant failed to unwrap her peanuts for her. This was possible only because of the power that this woman wielded by virtue of her father's *chaebol* position. The fact that nobody was able to refuse her demonstrates precisely how effective hierarchy, and particularly high socio-economic status, govern Koreans today.

### "We are *kkanbu*"

Intimacy and distance are constantly played with in *Squid Game*, and it can provide a glimpse into how Koreans build intimacy. It is an important part of daily life in Korea, and something that is often not transmitted in *K-*, with address terms used between fans to build solidarity rather than in negotiation of interpersonal relations. Subsequently, the hierarchical factors for deciding upon these terms are often made invisible in translation, so the way fans use these words is different.

*Jieun:* The word *kkanbu*, which was relatively unknown and unused by Koreans today, became popularised through *Squid Game*, when it is used by Il-nam during an emotional scene before Gi-hun left him to die. Il-nam seemingly gives up his life for Gi-hun by letting him cheat.

I interviewed 191 people about *Squid Game*, and the first word they remembered was *kkanbu*. The term was slang used in the 1970s, used specifically between gangsters, meaning 'friend', and the etymology still is unknown. Yet, via the vehicle of *Squid Game* the word has come out of obscurity and taken on a life of its own, under the umbrella of *K-*, meaning 'good friends' and with an emotional feeling, thanks to the emotional scene it was used in.

## "I ate steak already with my stepdad"

In one scene, in episode 1, Gi-hun takes his daughter for *ddeokbeoki*, when she admits to already having eaten dinner at a steak restaurant with her mother and stepfather. Gi-hun is hurt by this. The situation is definitive of the relationship he has with his daughter, who he has become, and the downtrodden feeling he has.

*Loli:* But, why steak?

*Jieun:* In Korea, the food you eat tells a lot about your social status, just like the etiquette, clothing, speaking English, and where you went to university. In this context, steak is used as a symbol of wealth, and stark contrast to what Gi-hun is providing: rice cakes with spicy sauce – a snack food. The situation is familiar too. In *Parasite* (2019), when the wealthy Mrs Park eats a snack – an inexpensive junk food ramen – she tops it with steak. In this respect, like everything else in Korean society, even food has a hierarchy. *Ddeokboki* is far from beef, and *dalgona* is far from *ddeokboki*.

## Oppa, hyeong, sajangnim

In *Squid Game*, address terms, like all other expressions of hierarchy and status, play a major role in dressing the sets, characters, and their interactions. They are a means of showing desperation, persuasion, status, emotions, and attitudes.

*Jieun:* Mi-nyeo, for instance, famously tries to negotiate for some form of protection from gangster Deok-su by calling him *oppa*, which was translated as 'old man' and 'babe' in a variety of translations, losing its precise Korean meaning related to intimacy and respect to create solidarity, agreeability, and flirtation, and the humour created due to Mi-nyeo's aged appearance.

*Loli:* *Hyeong* also was famously used in the heart-breaking scene in which Sang-woo tricks Abdul at the marble game, after gaining his trust, and Abdul calls out *hyeong* until he realises that Sang-woo has taken the marbles and left, and now Abdul will die. The emotional nuance that is created by the responsibility of Sang-woo as Abdul's *hyeong* 'older brother' to protect him can't be equated, even though the sadness of the betrayal is still conveyed on universal terms.

*Jieun:* Also, the use of *sajangnim* 'manager' by Abdul to Koreans shows his immigrant status and contains nuance about the discrimination and abuse of power that he has endured during his time in Korea, putting forward his cause as quite a noble one, especially in comparison to many of the other contestants who arrived there by means of their misdeeds and depravity.

A sizable portion of the immigrant population in Korea is made up of temporary labourers. Following Korea's economic boom, many members of the younger generation became less willing to work in '3D' jobs: jobs deemed dangerous, dirty, or demeaning, such as factory or farm work. This led to an uptake in immigrants from poorer countries, particularly countries in South or Southeast Asia, who came to fill the gaps left by Korean citizens. Legal migrant workers are typically employed on three-year visas, and extensions require consent and sponsorship by their employer. While in Korea, migrant workers cannot change jobs, lest they invalidate their visa.

*Emily:* These migrants are vastly different from the educated and sophisticated foreigners that have often been represented in Korean television shows.

*Bijeongsanghoedam* (비정상회담) 'Abnormal Summit' (also known as 'Non-Summit') is a prime example. Shows like this in the early 2000s featured foreign panellists that are all highly skilled in the Korean language and well educated. *Abnormal Summit* featured a panel of foreign members, modelled after the G20 summit. Many panellists lived in Korea as graduate or doctoral students, while others ran a wide gamut of careers, including professional gamer, trainees for K-pop groups, diplomats, and businessmen. Moreover, 11 of the 24 panellists in the show's run have hailed from Western countries in Europe or North America. Additionally, visiting 'intern' representatives would partake in debates for one or two episodes, either to replace absent regular members, or to add new viewpoints and diversity to the cast. Each week, the foreign members debate a topic submitted by viewers, and discuss whether the viewpoint represented by the viewer is 'normal' or 'abnormal'. These questions are largely related to Korean culture and life in Korea, and the regular members are often joined by celebrity guests.

 *Abnormal Summit* embodies the emphasis Korea places on attracting highly skilled foreign workers. These successful foreign panellists, with superior Korean skills, represent a push towards *damunhwa* (다문화), or multiculturalism, and a more globalised Korea. Additionally, by having panellists discuss the viewpoints and idiosyncrasies of their home countries, Korean viewers are exposed to a wider range of cultures and identities.

 *Abnormal Summit* does not paint the full picture of immigration in Korea. More specifically, it does not accurately represent who is immigrating. Although there are many migrant workers in Korea legally on temporary work visas, there are an even larger number who are undocumented. It is estimated that 400,000 undocumented migrant workers reside in Korea, in addition to the 250,000 documented workers.[17] These undocumented workers may enter Korea on a three-month tourist visa and overstay their visa to work or may have entered with a work visa that has since expired.

The plight of migrants is highlighted in *Squid Game* by the character of Pakistani migrant worker Ali Abdul, and North Korean defector Sae-byeok. Abdul's character is reflective of the struggles that migrant workers face. In one scene, Abdul is shown arguing with his employer over unpaid wages. His employer has been able to get away with this because of Abdul's desperate situation. He is shown living in a cramped apartment with his wife and young child. The situation between him and his employer escalates to violence, putting Abdul and his family into a dire set of circumstances, due to which he is then desperate enough to enter the game.

In the show, even among the array of degenerates who have entered the game, there is a clear social divide between migrant workers and Korean citizens, with migrant workers finding themselves at a disadvantage. The divide felt and experienced by Abdul, for instance, is shown in his submissive behaviour towards all whom he meets. It is made abundantly clear in the language he uses, both verbal and non-verbal. He uses the address term *sajangnim*, which means 'manager', to address the male contestants, showing them respect indiscriminately. Because of the environment that the term belongs to, the use of *sajangnim* also shows that Abdul is a factory worker, indicating the type of experience he will have had in Korea – low pay, long working hours, and isolation from the Korean society. His frequent nodding, bowing, and use of two hands when giving and receiving are also reflective of the higher respect that he is used to showing towards Koreans in general, which is significantly more than what we observe between the Korean characters, who, if anything, drop formality entirely due to the extreme situation. Elements like this that are woven into the show highlight the social divide that exists in reality between migrant workers and Korean citizens.

Sae-byeok, on the other hand, is hardened by her experience of being an immigrant. She is cold, aggressive, and will not agree to bond with anyone. This can be mistaken as being purely because of her experience escaping North Korea, but if we consider the 'desperate circumstances' that generally lead to this kind of immigration, Abdul and Sae-byeok are similar. The difference is how they deal with their circumstances – criminality versus overworking and underpay – though ultimately both amount to slavery. Both characters are manipulated by Korean citizens because of their desperation. They are abused financially and taunted with the things that they need by those in power to keep control over them. Sae-byeok was offered work by local criminal organisations who didn't help her as they promised and by brokers whose services she obtained to try to grant her other family members safe passage to South Korea.

Korea's "education fever" has led to a dramatic increase in the number of Korean citizens completing a university education, who are then reluctant to enter this 3D workforce. The labour shortage has led to factory or farm owners turning to other countries to supply workers. Although migrant workers are desperately needed to support Korea's economy, they often suffer from low quality of life, and even documented workers don't always receive the support they need from the government when it comes to unpaid wages or other rights abuses. Poor conditions for migrant workers and immigration raids to deport undocumented workers have often led to protests by activist groups and worker unions to fight for fair treatment of migrant workers.

## Notes

1 Douglas, Nicole. 2021. "Netflix is SUED by South Korean Internet Provider Over Traffic Spike from Squid Game." *Daily Mail Australia*. https://www.dailymail.co.uk/tvshowbiz/article-10056067/Netflix-sued-Squid-Game-causes-surge-viewers-South-Korea.html
2 Richwine, Lisa. 2022. "'Squid Game' Grabs Early Emmy Awards, Setting up Drama Battle." www.reuters.com/lifestyle/squid-game-grabs-early-emmy-awards-setting-up-drama-battle-2022-09-05/
3 Kaur, Brahmjot. 2022. "Lee Jung-Jae of 'Squid Game' Made History with Emmy for Best Actor in Drama: He's the First Actor from a Non-English Show to Win the Award." *NBC News*. www.bbc.co.uk/news/entertainment-arts-62796137
4 Kwon, Mee-yoo. 2020. "'Parasite' Subtitle Translator Becomes Busan Honorary Citizen." *The Korea Times*. www.koreatimes.co.kr/www/art/2020/04/689_288258.html
5 Slugfo. 2022. "Red Light, Green Light." *Roblox*. www.roblox.com/games/7540891731/Red-Light-Green-Light
6 LeGardye, Q. 2021. "The 'Squid Game' Games Are Based on Real-Life Children's Games: The Korean and International Games Have Taken Over Social Media." *Marie Claire*.
7 Kim, V. 2021. "The Seedy World of Private Lending in 'Squid Game' is a Real Temptation in South Korea." *Los Angeles Times*. www.latimes.com/world-nation/story/2021-10-16/the-seedy-world-of-private-lending-in-squid-game-is-a-real-temptation-in-todays-south-korea
8 Jung, J. 2017. "Inside the World of Korea's Loan Sharks." *Korea JoongAng Daily*. https://koreajoongangdaily.joins.com/2017/08/14/finance/Inside-the-world-of-Koreas-loan-sharks/3037143.html
9 Lee, Y. 2020. "Seo Jung-jin: Founder Who Needed Loan Sharks is Now South Korea's Second Richest." *The Economic Times*. https://economictimes.indiatimes.com/news/international/world-news/seo-jung-jin-founder-who-needed-loan-sharks-is-now-south-koreas-second-richest/articleshow/77099032.cms?utm_source=contentofinterest&utm_medium=text&utm_campaign=cppst
10 Kim, Victoria. 2021. "The Seedy World of Private Lending in 'Squid Game' is a Real Temptation in South Korea." *Los Angeles Times*. www.latimes.com/world-nation/story/2021-10-16/the-seedy-world-of-private-lending-in-squid-game-is-a-real-temptation-in-todays-south-korea
11 Jung, J. 2017. "Inside the World of Korea's Loan Sharks." *Korea JoongAng Daily*. https://koreajoongangdaily.joins.com/2017/08/14/finance/Inside-the-world-of-Koreas-loan-sharks/3037143.html

12 Wang, Mei, and Cho sujin. 2018. "A Comparative Study of Korean-Chinese Leave Home Novel in the Period of Industrialization and Reform and Opening-up – Centering on the Works of Hwang Seok-Young and Chen Yingsong." *Journal of North-East Asian Cultures*, 1(56), pp. 105–127. https://doi.org/10.17949/jneac.1.56.201809.007

13 Mirjalili, Fatemeh. 2021. "The Labor Strike Flashback in Squid Game is Based on a Real Tragic Event in Korean History." *Slash Film*. www.slashfilm.com/653766/the-labor-strike-flashback-in-squid-game-is-based-on-a-real-tragic-event-in-korean-history/?utm_campaign=clip

14 Choi, Sung-jin. 2015. "'Spoon Class Theory' Gains Force in Korea." *The Korea Times*. www.koreatimes.co.kr/www/tech/2018/11/693_191159.html

Kim, Hyejin. 2017. "'Spoon Theory' and the Fall of a Populist Princess in Seoul." *Journal of Asian Studies*, 76(4), pp. 839–849. https://doi.org/10.1017/S0021911817000778

15 Choi, Hayoung, and Ju-min Park. 2019. "Wider Image: No Money, No Hope: South Korea's 'Dirt Spoons' Turn against Moon." *Reuters*. www.reuters.com/article/us-southkorea-politics-dirtspoon-idUSKBN1Y02MK

16 Choe, Sang-Hun. 2018. "Sister of Korean 'Nut Rage' Heiress Accused of Throwing Her Own Tantrum." *The New York Times*. www.nytimes.com/2018/04/13/world/asia/nut-rage-sister-korean-air.html

17 Ock, Hyun-Ju. 2020, September 29. "[Feature] No Jobs, No Flights Home: Migrant Workers Stranded in S. Korea." *The Korea Herald*. www.koreaherald.com/view.php?ud=20200929000735

Stokes, Monet. 2021, January 28. "Migrants Are Doing the Jobs South Koreans Sneer At." *Foreign Policy. The Slate Group*. https://foreignpolicy.com/2021/01/28/south-korea-migrant-workers/

# 3

# *PARASITE*

Bong Joon-ho's *Gisaengchung* (기생충) 'Parasite' (2019) was the catalyst that brought on Hallyu 3.0, when it broke new ground for Asia in its positive reception among global audiences, especially Western audiences. *Parasite* received a long list of awards from Hollywood – despite its notorious elusiveness for international filmmakers. Moreover, the awards include some of the most prestigious; among them four Academy Awards, a Golden Globe, and two BAFTAs in 2020. Perhaps the most significant was *Parasite* becoming the first non-English film to win Best Picture, and Bong Joon-ho becoming the first South Korean to win Best Director. Parasite's big wins enabled Korean film – and subsequently the K-Wave – to find firm footing on Hollywood turf; enough that a domino effect of Western engagement and popularity ensued, which facilitated the K-Wave's move into the mainstream. *Parasite*'s reception was very much the signifier of a greater cultural shift, in which Korea's soft power has begun to rival the traditionally dominant Anglophone-Western films, not only competing but helping to create a new model for economic success that is more diverse and culturally rich.

*Jieun:* The first time I saw *Parasite*, I recognised so much that I had experienced first-hand. I was an au pair when I was a student in Seoul, and I was so shocked because the Park family's house is so much like the house of the French couple that I worked for. I looked after their daughter after school and sometimes when her parents went to parties. The family had household staff too, just like the Park family, including a cook.

Their modern house was situated in a French area that looked a lot like the Park family's neighbourhood. The area is called Seolmal, and many French residents live there, as well as *chaebol*. It is attractive to live in these wealthy foreign districts, where foreign ambassadors and company CEOs

DOI: 10.4324/9781003203230-3

live. The father was CEO of a French company based in Seoul. There are
many areas like this, such as Seorae Maeul (French town), Youngsan (where
retired foreign military officers reside), and there is a German village too.
Itaewon is another district known for foreigners; however, this region is not
synonymous with luxury but the opposite thanks to the foreign soldiers and
tourists who frequent the area's rowdy nightlife. This division of foreign
and local districts, like the poor and wealthy districts, makes Seoul appear
ghettoised and provides the landscape in which *Parasite* unfolds.

### Banjiha

We begin our selection of objects with the Kim family's infamous semi-basement
apartment – the *'banjiha'* (반지하) – known for their low rents and poor living conditions, and considered at the bottom of South Korean real estate.[1] These
apartments lack space and light and are reported as being damp, with little privacy.
Bong Joon-ho's production designer, Lee Ha-jun, visited and photographed towns
due to be torn down and used this to design the Kim family's street and *banjiha*
set. In an interview with IndieWire, Lee Ha-jun explained the choice to put the
Kim family in a *banjiha* stating, "I didn't add that to just show a very Korean
element of the story. There's a more specific meaning behind it because the semi-
basement is basically in the middle of high and low. There's this fear that you can
fall even further below but you still feel hope that you're still half above-ground,
so it really reflects this liminal space that they're in, and the spaces in this film
are even more compartmentalized and all connected through a very complicated
staircase."[2]

But *banjiha* are not just an idiosyncrasy of Korean architecture; there is much
more to them than that. They are the upshot of Korea's history and are richly symbolic. Their origins go all the way back to South Korea's conflict with North Korea,
decades ago. In 1970, following an assassination attempt on President Park Chung-
hee in 1968, multiple infiltrations by North Korean commandos, numerous terrorist
incidents, and the attack and capture of a US Navy ship by North Korea, the South
Korean government changed building codes so that low-rise apartment complexes
required basements. Should the situation escalate, and a national emergency arise,
the plan was for them to be used as bunkers.

In the beginning, renting out a *banjiha* was illegal. However, when the housing
crisis hit in the 1980s, the government decided to change this. Seoul is incredibly
cramped, with 25.6 million people – half of South Korea's population – residing
there,[3] making housing extremely unaffordable. The BBC recently reported that the
rent-to-income ratio for tenants under 35 years of age has remained at roughly 50%
for the past ten years, so with monthly rent at a *banjiha* being on average 540,000
Korean won (roughly £345), and average monthly salaries of Koreans in their 20s
being around 2,000,000 won (roughly £1,279), the *banjiha* has become a means for
these lower income households to maintain a residence in Seoul.

*Jieun:* Seoul was expanded, but it still wasn't enough. There are still areas in need of modernisation, cramped with properties like these.

The World Population Review (2022) reported that "Rapid urban growth has resulted in various problems for South Korea. High-rise apartments were constructed to help alleviate housing shortages, but this also caused severe hardship on the thousands of people who were forced to relocate from their old neighbourhoods since they were unable to afford the rent in the new buildings. In the late 1980s, squatter areas which contained one-story shacks still existed in different parts of Seoul. Housing for most of the population, bar the wealthiest, was generally cramped."

*Banjiha* were first brought to the attention of the masses when *Parasite* hit the screens, and of the many objects of global interest, it got audiences talking. Then in 2022, floods in Seoul, brought on by the heaviest rainfall in South Korea in decades, brought the *banjiha* to the attention of mainstream media once again. The streets of Seoul's affluent Gangnam district were turned into rivers, with cars submerged in water, leaving roads severely damaged and flooding tube stations. Al Jazeera (2022) reported that "At least eight people were killed, and seven others reported missing". BBC News reported that, in one case, two women in their 40s and a 13-year-old girl were found dead in their *banjiha*, after getting trapped there during the flood.[4]

The devastation caused by the floods was reminiscent of that depicted by Bong Joon-ho in *Parasite*, which it could be argued placed even greater spotlight on the disaster, with mainstream media referring to *Parasite* while talking about the disaster. The Korean government was urged by officials to act, and there is now a plan to revise the building law to ban *banjiha* for residential purposes. *Banjiha* owners will be given 20 years to convert them for non-residential purposes (e.g., parking),

**FIGURE 3.1** 2022 floods in Seoul, South Korea.

FIGURE 3.2    Mr Kim arrives home to find he no longer has one, and everything he owns is immersed in water, in *Parasite*.

while there is talk of provisions for *banjiha* tenants to help them to access other forms of housing.

Now we spend some time deconstructing some of the smaller objects that compose the *banjiha*, which is presented in a similar format to the Park family's house that is presented directly after the 'Banjiha' section, in order for insightful comparisons to be drawn.

### Neighbourhood

The neighbourhood of the *banjiha* is very much a part of the *banjiha* in that both are grains of the low-income ecosystem in Seoul. People who can only afford to live in *banjiha* reside in a less desirable neighbourhood and, as such, have lifestyles and backgrounds in common. You wouldn't expect to see a mansion on the same street as a *banjiha*; therefore, you wouldn't expect to find a chaebol CEO living in such a neighbourhood, nor would you expect to find the finest restaurants situated there – they simply are not in alignment with 'what is offered' and 'for whom'.

*Loli:* What do you feel about the connection between neighbourhood and one's identity in Korea regarding *Parasite*?

*Jieun:* The social message throughout *Parasite* is expressed through the architecture, both characters' homes (e.g., Mr Kim's *banjiha*, and Mr Park's house) and the related neighbourhood structures, streets, and their facilities. There is a clear link made to the identity of the characters. The streets of the poor neighbourhood are cluttered and cramped just like the *banjiha*, while the rich have spacious homes and spacious streets.

*Loli:* Then the characters themselves embody characteristics associated with the status that their environments reflect. Take Mrs Park, for instance. Her

**FIGURE 3.3**    Narrow, cluttered streets nearby the *banjiha*, in *Parasite*.

expensive clothing, her little dogs, her use of customs, and yet at the same time her discretion to forget about etiquette when she feels like it. She places her feet on the back of the passenger car seat when Mr Kim is driving her, but then when she communicates with Ki-woo (her daughter's English tutor who she values greatly), she hands him his payment in a white envelope, showing respect to him. Likewise, she uses deferential hand gestures like placing her hands together in her lap, leaning forward slightly, and adopting polite speech with Ki-woo. In this case she feels proper etiquette is warranted. It is all related to her status.

Loli:    The restaurant where the Kim family is shown eating is for taxi drivers to eat their fill affordably. Mr Park would be unwelcomed there certainly. Not only is he not a taxi driver, but he is not welcome to this hospitality, which is reserved for working-class men in need of a substantial meal at a good price. The Kim family are so poverty-stricken that they are able to eat there without even raising an eyebrow, and this is before Mr Kim takes up his role as the Park family's driver.

Jieun:    It may seem strange to non-Koreans, and especially in places like the UK, where you find more affluent areas nearby those less so. Likewise, the places people eat and work are often intermingled. In the UK and US, for instance, even if you're rich, you can go to McDonalds, and nobody cares. But, in Korea people would likely stare and want you to leave.

### 'Temple of excrement' and sleeping mat

Returning to the interview with IndieWire, Lee Ha-jun also stated that in the script the bathroom in the *banjiha* was named "the temple of excrement" by Bong Joon-ho, which Lee Ha-jun designed using a combination of consideration for camera angles and inspiration from his college days, during which he lived in a *banjiha* that he claims had a bathroom just like this.

**FIGURE 3.4**   The *banjiha* bathroom, in *Parasite*.

A re-creation of the *banjiha* bathroom in *Parasite* was recently displayed at the *Hallyu! The Korean Wave* exhibition at the V&A Museum in London. This example justifies our argument that these objects are elements of *K-* under the umbrella of each film or show, through which their everydayness is transformed into the spectacular; a *banjiha* bathroom is indicative of status in Korea and nothing more, but for non-Koreans signifies *Parasite* and meanings associated with it, and is believed to be of such importance that it features in an exhibition of a world-renowned museum.

The rooms in the *banjiha* are just as cramped as the bathroom. Their space for sleeping is limited. Each of two bedrooms has a pile of thick blankets for sleeping on, and a traditional sleeping mat can be seen on the floor of Mr and Mrs Kim's room. These blankets are folded into a pile upon waking each day and then prepared again each night, so that the room can be used for other purposes in the day. This is not unusual. Many Koreans use this more traditional method of sleeping. However, as we show in contrast, the wealthy often opt for Western beds as a symbol of status, as it reflects their financial ability to purchase imported goods, and their social mobility in their knowledge of Western culture (like the status acquired by speaking English).

In *Hanyeo* (하녀) 'The Housemaid' (2010), protagonist Eun-yi, who goes to work as a housemaid in a wealthy house, has a Western bed, so, it isn't impossible to see this outside of wealthy households. It is, however, important to highlight the difference between a bed seen in cheap accommodation and those found in wealthy homes. Eun-yi's bed is more of a mattress than a bed. It doesn't have a frame or a headboard. Moreover, it is a large single bed, and she shares it with her friend, in a single room that they rent together. Though the form of housing and furnishings are slightly different, Eun-yi's room is so cramped that there is little room to stand around the bed which reflects her low status.

## *Window*

Our next object is the window. Bong Joon-ho repeatedly talks of the importance of light in creating a contrast between the lives of the rich and poor in *Parasite*, and he deliberately uses natural lighting to achieve this. Returning to his interview with IndieWire, Bong Joon-ho explained, "Because the story is about the rich and poor, that's obviously the approach we had to take in terms of designing the sound and lighting. The poorer you are, the less sunlight you have access to, and that's just how it is in real life as well: you have a limited access to windows. For example, in *Snowpiercer*, the tail cars didn't have any windows and with semi-basement homes, you have a very limited amount of sunlight you get during the day – maybe 15 or 30 minutes – and that's where the film opens."

The windows in *Parasite* are the unsung heroes of Bong Joon-ho's achievements with lighting, however. The natural light that falls through the small, ground-level windows of the *banjiha* contrast with the light flooding through the windows of Mr Park's house. One window even takes up the entirety of the living room wall, replacing a television so that the Parks observe their garden instead. Since the sets were custom built, contrasting window sizes were maximised upon.

The Kim family also doesn't have a television, and they also appear to observe what goes on through the window, with that becoming their topic of discussion or entertainment. Like the Park household, the windows show much more than light, all of which is related to status and identity. The *banjiha* windows offer glimpses of the deprivation of society. In the daytime bug exterminators walk through the streets spraying gas to kill the insects that flourish in this poorer side of town, and the Kim family are overcome by smoke in their house, to which they can only respond by covering their mouths with their t-shirts and fanning the room.

In the evenings, their home is assaulted on a regular basis by the vomiting and urination of local drunks, a common occurrence due to the drinking culture in

FIGURE 3.5   The window is the Park family's television, and expensive abstract art hangs on the wall, in *Parasite*.

FIGURE 3.6    The *banjiha* window in *Parasite*. An exterminator sprays insect repellent, and it seeps through the window, overwhelming *banjiha* inhabitants.

Korea. In 2016, Al Jazeera reported that "South Korea is also home to more alcoholics than any other country, and alcohol-related social costs amount to more than $20bn a year, Ministry of Health and Welfare estimates show."[5]

*Loli:*    Interestingly, the lowest level of the Parks' house – the underground bunker – is perhaps the closest aesthetically to the *banjiha*. The dishevelled walls, cramped space, narrow corridors, and unhygienic toilet area not so different from the "temple of excrement" that Bong Joon-ho described the Kim family's bathroom.[6] The primary difference between the Kim family's semi-basement apartment and the bunker is that they have some light at least provided by their limited number of small ground-level windows, and their facilities are a little better.

### From low to high – from poor to rich

When Ki-woo goes for his interview with Mrs Park for the role of her daughter's English tutor, we are presented with an interesting sequence of scenes from his journey, as he travels across the boundary of one neighbourhood into another; clearly defined by the social status of their inhabitants. In their interview with *Architectural Digest*, Lee Ha-jun explained their depiction of contrasts like the ones made in this sequence:[7]

Mr Park's house is minimal, uncluttered, large and orderly. It's a large house with a large garden consisting of controlled colours and materials – a contrast to the semi-basement neighbourhood. In contrast to the rich house, Kitaek's semi-basement neighbourhood is more colourful, but again, we minimized the colour tones as much as possible so that no particular tone stood out. Instead, the textures are rough and the space is denser compared to the rich house. I wanted to show the increasing density that reflects the class difference between elevated

**FIGURE 3.7**  Ki-woo exits the entrance to his family's *banjiha* (exterior), in *Parasite*.

areas and lower ones as appearances change from the rich house to the semi-basement neighbourhood. This is a story about co-existence, but both Director Bong and I were certain that we had to show clear contrast as well. That contrast is maximized in how the appearance of the neighbourhood gradually changes when the family endlessly descends from top to bottom.

Here, we examine that sequence, including the entrances of both residences, and a glimpse into the neighbourhoods surrounding.

### Entrance

As Ki-woo exits his *banjiha*, he is shown passing through the narrow, cluttered hallway. Even when he reaches the front doorway, his mother can be seen crouching on the ground cleaning something on the other side.

### Neighbourhood

As he passes his mother, continuing down a narrow passageway to the street, the lack of space and clutter continues.

When he arrives at the Park family's neighbourhood, the landscape architecture is the polar opposite to his neighbourhood. Houses are enclosed behind high walls, some lush with green vegetation. Roads are winding, clean, and uphill, suggesting that it is physically higher up than in his neighbourhood where the street is level.

### Entrance

Finally, Ki-woo locates the Park family's house and introduces himself over the intercom at a very different entrance to the one he first emerged from. He is buzzed in, and the door opens on its own. Ki-woo appears a little surprised by this and

**FIGURE 3.8**    Ki-woo arrives at the Park family's affluent neighbourhood, in *Parasite*.

**FIGURE 3.9**    Ki-woo enters the house through an entrance very different to that of his *banjiha*, in *Parasite*.

unsure of the situation. He finally approaches the door and peers through for a moment before entering. The entrance area he is standing in is generously sized, and this he finds is the entrance to an outdoor area rather than the house.

The door leads to a set of stairs, surrounded by more plant life. When he reaches the top, he finds himself in a garden – an open green space, framed by shapely bushes. The camera pans 360°, which emphasises the sense of overwhelming size. The house standing before Ki-woo is large and modern. At the front is another large entryway, where the housekeeper, Mun-kwang, comes out to greet him.

*Jieun:* Having a garden in Seoul is very rare. People typically have a balcony in their apartment and sometimes an apartment village has gardens surrounding it, but this is not something those on low incomes can afford. These days, having a garden is something for which people must go out of the capital, so having a garden in Seoul signifies their wealth. Therefore, *chae-bol* in Korean films and dramas are often seen with gardens, not necessarily of a Western style. Just owning a simple lawn is symbolic.

Stepping inside of the residence, Ki-woo is greeted with more severe contrasts to his home. Compared to his own home's entryway, which is small, cluttered, and dark, the Park family's entryway is bright, with more glass than brick, a wide, spacious walkway, and an area for changing into house slippers, as per Korean etiquette norms.

We can observe similar architectural conventions in wealthy households depicted in other K-films and dramas too, so none of this is specifically down to the Park family's character or tastes. Returning to *The Housemaid* (2010), we see similarly high walls, a garden, and a large, spacious entryway there.

These are just a few of the objects significant in creating the socio-economic contrasts during Ki-woo's journey from his neighbourhood to the Park's is significant in marking his identity in contrast to the Parks' identities.

## The house with a garden

We have given a glimpse of the Park family's house and neighbourhood already, but now we elaborate further on some of the key objects within it. The Park family's house is where the action happens for most of the film, and like the *banjiha*, the house is a character itself in the film.

### Bath, bed, and art

In contrast to the Kim family's home, the Park family does not sleep on mats, and their bathroom is not cramped. They have modern Western furniture, including beds, and a luxurious bathtub. Even their children's rooms are large, spacious, and stylish. Although some of the items will be found commonly in Western homes, they are more affordable there because the items do not need to be imported.

*Loli:*  This is an element of the Korean context that is often lost through *K*-. The elements being interpreted and missed vary among viewers, and they generally tend to arrive at a similar understanding, but via different routes, and with subtle differences.

The Parks' rooms are completed with priceless art, which they use to show off. It is a status symbol. Bong Joon-ho featured actual famous works in the set. On the living room wall hangs a piece featuring a forest made from stainless steel wire mesh by Korean artist Seung-mo Park. The painting is from his series *Maya* (2011–2017). Seung-mo Park also created an original image of cats especially for the movie.

*Staircase*

Hierarchy is central in Korean society; everything is hierarchised because one must show their status as well as interpret that of other people. In *Parasite* (2019), stairs are symbols of the higher and lower rungs of society. They are symbolic of status, just as a garden is. Take the *banjiha*, for instance, it doesn't have a staircase, and it is the lowest and most undesirable residence in a building – all elements are pointed downwards. This occurs in the Korean language too: downward address terms and speech styles for speaking to inferiors, and upward address terms and speech styles for superiors. This same concept seems to manifest in the material world in Korean society. Returning to the interview in *Architectural Digest*, Lee Ha-jun touched on the subject:[8]

> There are actual houses with high walls and large gardens in elevated neigh-bourhoods of Seoul. But the staircase is one of the key visual elements of this film. Director Bong was very precise with his demand that everything must continue to descend from top to bottom. The appearance of the neighbourhoods had to gradually change. There had to be more rain and more water to complete the overall nuance and spatiality of the film. We did, however, struggle with the numerous staircases on location – the numerous power lines and staircases we see as the family comes down. Both Mr. Park's rich house and Kitaek's semi-basement house feature several staircases of varying size within the homes. They go up and go down. I've never created so many staircases while working on a film.

There are four staircases inside the Park family's house, and two sets of stairs outside of the house (one at the front and one at the rear), and they were certainly made good use of in the film. Scenes shot in the Parks' house were rarely without a staircase. Characters go up and down, and much of the action takes place on one of their staircases.

Bong Joon-ho explained that much of the house's design, including stairs, was to create the opportunity for certain scenes to take place how he imagined. For example, having the house with an open plan with the staircase visible and the kitchen beside it means that characters can be captured spying within a single frame. Bong wanted to capture the characters as they sneaked about, and the stairs were one way of doing this. It didn't have to be stairs that facilitated this, but to emphasise the contrast with the *banjiha*, they were well-suited.

*Loli:*  Kim Ki-young's Hanyeo (하녀) '*The Housemaid*' (1960) also employs the staircase as a symbol of status, along with a similar set of objects as the Parks do, only they are related to the era, which was the early days of the *chaebol* era, when families like the Parks didn't really exist yet. What can you tell us about the parallels between status and how it is used in the two films?

FIGURE 3.10   Da-song spies from the staircase on the adults' conversation in the kitchen, in *Parasite*.

FIGURE 3.11   Many of the family's interactions take place on or in front of the staircase in *The Housemaid* (1960).

*Jieun:*   I think the use of stairs in *Parasite* echoes back to *The Housemaid* (1960). There is so much parallel imagery used for the same purposes: the stairs – going up and down like *Parasite*, as well as the frequent action that takes place on them – and high-status foods, clothing, and pets.

*Loli:*   Interestingly, the modern remake of *The Housemaid* (2010) also emphasises stairs, and that there are separate staircases to take you to the family and staff quarters. There is a clear distinction between spaces, even when sharing the same home. The aesthetic of the staircases is entirely different – one being flamboyant and luxurious, and the other understated.

## A housewife's *hanbok*

There are a few further objects to point out in our discussion of the parallels between *Parasite* (2019) and *The Housemaid* (1960).

*Jieun:* Mrs Park in *Parasite* (2019) wears luxurious clothing – these are not clothes you would work in. Mrs Kim in *The Housemaid* (1960) also does so, only because of the period, this takes the form of a traditional *hanbok*. The *hanbok* is heavy and difficult to work in, and thus shows her status. Women who wear clothes that show status like this are addressed as *samonim* (사모 님) 'teacher's wife' in Korea, even by strangers, purely based on their fine clothing. This is a term which shows respect to a woman of higher status.

FIGURE 3.12    An image of status from the period that remains relevant today: Mrs Kim ascending the staircase wearing a *hanbok* in *The Housemaid* (1960).

FIGURE 3.13    Parallel image. Mrs Park walks up the stairs in *Parasite* wearing luxurious clothing but without *hanbok*.

*Loli:*  Why doesn't Mrs Park wear a *hanbok* to show her status?

*Jieun:*  The periodical factor is important when it comes to the hierarchy of objects. In the 1960s when *The Housemaid* (1960) was made, *hanbok* offered traditional status, which was considered sophisticated and thus high status. Women of status would wear less makeup with *hanbok* to achieve an elegant look. In recent years, the *hanbok* has become trendy in contemporary Korea. Young people want to wear it and participate in Korean culture, and through this, *hanbok* has lost some of these associations with high status.

### Ramdon

In one scene, Mrs Park asks her housekeeper to make what is referred to in the subtitle as '*ramdon*' – a term invented for the film by subtitle translator Darcy Paquet who felt *jjapaguri* was more difficult to infer quickly. *Ramdon* combines morphemes from well-known Japanese words for noodle – *ramen* and *udon*. *Jjapaguri* is a uniquely Korean dish, which consists of a combination of two noodle products – *chapagetti ramyeon* and the Chinese-inspired *jajang ramyeon*. *Jjapaguri* is not a high-class dish but rather a cheap snack food. Mrs Park makes it into something that surpasses any snack by adding high-quality beef to the dish. This is a marker of her status. Korean *hanwoo* beef is in limited supply, and as such it is costly. Mrs Park adding this expensive beef to *ramyeon* emphasises her wealth.

Thanks to Darcy Paquet's invention of the term '*ramdon*', *jjapaguri* plus steak is now a popularised dish around the world, which continues to be known by those who experienced the dish by engaging with *K-* as *ramdon*. Further, the participatory nature of the engagement with *ramdon* has led to further evolution of this element of *K-*.[9]

In *The Housemaid* (1960), status is shown in a similar way by the family eating 'curry rice'. The first contact Korea had with Westernisation was during the Joseon dynasty, in the 17th century when envoys sent to China encountered Western

FIGURE 3.14   Mrs Park eating *ramdon*, in *Parasite*.

FIGURE 3.15    Parallel image. The Kim family eating "curry rice" together in bed, in *The Housemaid* (1960).

missionaries. However, it was really following the Korean War (1950–1953), when US soldiers increased their presence in Korea, that Western culinary culture entered the country. Foods like white bread, wheat flour, butter, margarine, and mayonnaise, which hadn't been common in Korea, suddenly became widely accessible. Before this, Korea had contact with Japanised Western food, such as curry (made with a curry cube or powder). In the 1960s, Korean people thought of this food as a Western dish, something modern, and trendy. Curry rice, which is essentially curry sauce on top of rice (sometimes containing vegetables and possibly meat), is thus used in the same way as steak was used in *Parasite*.

As is the case in any place, the rare has always been desirable, expensive, and therefore, a symbol of status. In Korea, the cost of importing Western food and drink products can be extremely expensive, subsequently boosting the status of the people who buy them. A bottle of Western alcohol, such as French wine, Scottish whisky, or Russian vodka costs almost the equivalent to £80 per bottle. While in the UK, for instance, a bottle of standard wine can be bought for around £5 and whisky or vodka around £20 for popular brands. In Korea, department stores, such as the popular COEX mall in Seoul, have a food supermarket that sells ingredients more like what would be found in an average supermarket in the UK. However, the prices are considerably more, and the supermarket is a luxurious place to shop. We see Mrs Park shopping there in *Parasite*, as Mr Kim trails behind her pushing her trolley.

Alongside the rise of numerous Western restaurants in Korea, an array of popular Western-Korean fusion dishes have become part of the everyday contemporary culinary culture among young adults in Korea, for instance, carbonara rice cakes, which is a combination of carbonara pasta sauce and rice cakes, and an array of pizzas that incorporate popular Korean foods, such as the *kimchi* pizza or *bulgogi* pizza. In K-films, Western foods like these are often used to show high socio-economic status, expensive taste, and luxury.

*Jieun:* There is a food hierarchy – or food politics – in Korea. We discussed the hierarchy between beef and *ddoekboki* earlier, but everything has its place in the hierarchy. For instance, white rice is considered superior to flour. This is historically rooted in the period after the Korean War. In 1955, in order to save rice, the Korean government promoted products such as barley, flour, and instant *ramyeon* (which was invented in 1968), to avoid famine. Flour was provided by America, and it subsequently became a food of hard times. The attitude that "flour is not proper food" has remained ever since. For instance, today, if you go to a noodle restaurant, restaurants always give you a bowl of rice because noodles are made from flour, even though it is carb plus carb. This is because rice is thought of as real food and noodles are not.

*Loli:* My husband is the same. He always puts rice into the *ramyeon* soup at the end after eating the noodles!

*Jieun:* This makes me think of a funny family anecdote. In the late 1980s, my dad was one of the few people who went to the US. One of the Koreans he travelled with took kimchi. They took it on board, and it burst during the flight. In a hotel room in the US the next day, they used an instant cooker to make *doenjang jjigae* (된장찌개) 'soybean soup'. They set off the fire alarm and were all kicked out of the hotel. They wanted their own food, because of the hierarchy they felt existed, so they couldn't eat Western food. My mother recalls this incident and having to find another place to stay.

## Fruit

Now we turn our attention to fruit. The conceptualisation of fruit in Korea is somewhat different than in the West. It is commonly eaten following meals, when one has visitors at their home, and fruit baskets are even given as a gift on traditional holidays to family, friends, and colleagues. There is a whole industry for fruit gift boxes in Korea, and sales have even increased in recent years.

*Loli:* We see gifts of fruit often in Korean television and cinema, and the growing of gourmet fruit and the giving of this fruit as gifts is something that extends across East Asia. In season 1, episode 2 of *Pachinko* (2022), which is an Apple TV+ original, we see Solomon trying to persuade an elderly Korean woman to sell her land in Tokyo. He brings her an expensive square-shaped watermelon, wrapped in a luxury box with a bow.

*Jieun:* We don't have tea culture in Korea, nor is there traditionally a dessert culture. We eat fruit after meals and as a quality snack. For instance, in Korea, when university students or graduates tutor elementary schoolchildren to earn some extra money, mums prepare fruit as a snack. When I was a tutor once, a mum brought me *mandu* (dumplings) to eat while teaching. Mums understand that students might not have a lot of money and might get hungry while teaching. The mum who gave me dumplings never thought of it as a meal, even though it was quite filling. She just considered it a decent snack. When it comes to fruit as a snack, in Korea, one mustn't underestimate the value of a single piece. A simple piece of fruit can be quite expensive.

## University certificate

Our next object is the university certificate. In *Parasite*, when Ki-woo's friend asks him to take over his tutoring role in the Park family's household, Ki-woo immediately sets a plan in action to prepare for successfully getting the role. He has his sister forge a degree certificate from Yonsei University, which is one of the top universities in Korea that has similar status as Oxford or Cambridge University in the UK and Harvard University in the US. The certificate is important because Yonsei University grants Ki-woo the kind of status needed to gain the respect of the Park family. When they show Mr Kim the finished certificate, he jokingly asks if Yonsei University has a degree in document forgery. In the subtitles, however, Yonsei is changed to Oxford to make the status translatable to non-Koreans.

*Jieun:* Education is such an important thing. Instances of forged degrees or certificates or other credentials occur often, which is evidence of how education is considered in Korea. In 2019, the daughter of a prominent political figure in South Korea (Cho Kuk) and her parents were accused of falsifying her academic achievements in order to enrol at prestigious universities and medical school. English and education, and preferably education outside of Korea at an English language university, are paramount.

*Loli:* We see how education and success are seen as status. When Ki-woo goes to the Parks' house for his interview, he pauses and looks at the pictures hanging on the wall. Large family portraits – also a symbol of status in Korea and very common – hang there, amongst which are some framed award certificates and newspaper articles celebrating Mr Park's success. In comparison, on the Kims' wall we see an old medal for shot put in a cheap frame, alongside a photo of Mrs Kim, seemingly as a youth, throwing the shot put.

## Scholar's Rock

We end this chapter on a symbolic note with the Scholar's Rock. Ki-woo's friend Min gave the Kim family the Scholar's Rock as a gift. It was somewhat ominous,

**FIGURE 3.16**  The Scholar's Rock is in pride of place, in the background of the Kim family's daily meals, in *Parasite*.

and Bong Joon-ho admitted that the choice was purposely strange.[10] It was first given to him by his grandfather, who told him that the stone will give him good luck and wealth. He hoped that it could give this to the Kim family. Ultimately, however, the Kim family meet their doom in a bittersweet cycle that is not unfamiliar in K-film.

*Jieun:*  People always remember this rock. Some people in Korean households have these, though it is not very common. They are often kept in a display case. They are known to fetch a lot at Korean auctions.
*Loli:*  Where do Scholar's Rocks originate from?
*Jieun:*  Scholar's Rocks are a Joseon dynasty tradition.

The Scholar's Rock sits near the Kim family's dining table until their *banjiha* is destroyed by floods. While they talk around the table at mealtimes, it can always be seen in the background. Then, late in the film, when the *banjiha* floods, the family return and try to save their belongings. Ki-woo only saves the Scholar's Rock during the flood. To people with money, the stone would mean nothing, but for the Kims, it is the only thing they have of worth. Ki-woo believes in the power of the rock. He even hugs it and says that it is attached to him and controlling him. This is a way of him blaming the stone for what is happening.

The day after the flood, the Kims go to the Parks' house for their son's birthday party. Ki-woo takes the rock, and holds it, traumatised by what has happened. As Mun-kwang's husband comes to take revenge for his wife's death, it is this same rock that he hits Ki-woo over the head with.

At the end of the film, Ki-woo recovers and acquires enough money to purchase the Park's old house. Before moving into the house, he returns the Scholar's Rock to the stream. It is a cycle: it started with the Scholar's Rock and ended with it. But

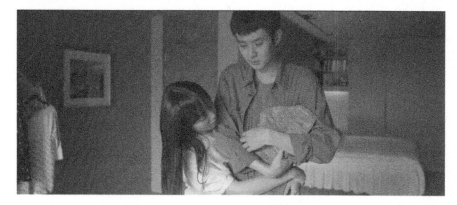

FIGURE 3.17    When he returns to the Park's household for their son's birthday party, Ki-woo takes the rock, believing it is playing a role in the events unfolding, in *Parasite*.

the Scholar's Rock has remained a mysterious object that people remember, talk about, and know the name of, even if they have little knowledge of what precisely it is or how to contextualise its use or purpose in *Parasite*.

*We end this chapter on the Scholar's Rock, paying homage to* Parasite, *which has given us so much these past years.*

## Notes

1   BBC. 10 February 2020. "Parasite: The Real People Living in Seoul's Basement Apartments." www.bbc.co.uk/news/world-asia-51321661; World Population Review. 2020. "South Korea Population." https://worldpopulationreview.com/countries/south-korea-population
2   O'Falt, Chris. 29 October 2019. "Building the 'Parasite' House: How Bong Joon Ho and His Team Made the Year's Best Set." *IndieWire*. www.indiewire.com/2019/10/parasite-house-set-design-bong-joon-ho-1202185829/
3   World Population Review. 2022. "Seoul Population 2022." https://worldpopulationreview.com/world-cities/seoul-population
4   Al Jazeera. 2022. "Photos: Eight Dead after Heavy Rains Cause Major Floods in Seoul." *Al Jazeera*. www.aljazeera.com/gallery/2022/8/9/photos-eight-dead-after-heavy-rains-cause-major-floods-in-seoul
5   Al Jazeera. 2016. "The Country with the World's Worst Drink Problem: South Korea Has More Alcoholics than Any Other Country, But It Seems Unlikely to Quit the Drink Any Time Soon." *Al Jazeera*. www.aljazeera.com/features/2016/2/7/the-country-with-the-worlds-worst-drink-problem
6   O'Falt, Chris. 29 October 2019. "Building the 'Parasite' House: How Bong Joon Ho and His Team Made the Year's Best Set." *IndieWire*. www.indiewire.com/2019/10/parasite-house-set-design-bong-joon-ho-1202185829/
7   Wallace, Rachel. 2019. "Inside the House from Bong Joon Ho's Parasite." *Architectural Digest*. www.architecturaldigest.com/story/bong-joon-ho-parasite-movie-set-design-interview

8  Wallace, Rachel. 2019. "Inside the House from Bong Joon Ho's Parasite." *Architectural Digest*. www.architecturaldigest.com/story/bong-joon-ho-parasite-movie-set-design-interview

9  A *ramdon* variation with vegetables: https://bestofkorea.com/next-level-ramdon-the-quintessential-high-low-dish-from-parasite/
   Halal *ramdon*: www.havehalalwilltravel.com/halal-ramdon-parasite-jinjja-chicken-singapore
   Food hall serving *ramdon* describes it as "Inspired by the movie 'Parasite,' our *Steak Ramdon* is stir-fried noodles with black bean paste and gochujang sauce, topped with grilled beef tenderloin.": https://thegridfoodmarket.com/products/steak-ramdon
   Takeaway *ramdon* available at The BIG Group: https://m.facebook.com/TheBigGroup/photos/a.264184456930276/3350892394926118/?type=3&_rdr

10 Brzeski, Patrick. 2020. "Bong Joon Ho Reveals the Significance of 'Parasite's' Scholar Stone." *The Hollywood Reporter*. www.hollywoodreporter.com/news/general-news/bong-joon-ho-reveals-significance-parasites-scholar-stone-1265811/

# 4

## *SKY CASTLE*

The popular satirical black comedy *SKY Kaeseul* (스카이캐슬) 'SKY Castle' (2018) shines a light on many of the subjects we see in *Parasite* (2019). It especially gives focus to the lengths that wealthy families will go to get their children into Korea's top universities, which is considered as important to their social status as it is to the wellbeing of their children.

*Jieun:* K-dramas like *SKY Castle* provide a way for viewers to learn about Korean education and its role in social mobility and cultural capital; for it is these concepts that underlie the objects placed within the camera frame in films like *Parasite*, and often which become *K-*.

*Emily:* If we begin with the title of the drama itself, it is a nod to the most prestigious and most highly sought-after universities in Korea, which are known by Koreans as 'SKY' universities. It is these universities that the Park family in *Parasite* are aiming at for their children's futures when they acquire tutors like Ki-woo and Ki-jung.

There are three SKY universities: Seoul National University (SNU), Korea University, and Yonsei University. These three universities, all located in Seoul, are culturally equivalent to the Ivy League in the US or the Golden Triangle in the UK. Admission to and graduation from these universities is believed to guarantee a good job and future financial success.

*Emily:* In the drama, the condominium complex that the wealthy characters inhabit is even called *SKY Castle* and is reserved only for the most elite doctors, lawyers, and professors in Korean society.

DOI: 10.4324/9781003203230-4

Much of the story revolves around Han Seo-jin, whose motivations and activities are parallel with Mrs Park's in *Parasite*, and her daughter Kang Ye-seo. The Kang family is known for educational excellence, and is aiming for three generations of doctors, relying on Ye-seo's acceptance to SNU. To guarantee her daughter's success, Seo-jin hires an expensive and exclusive private tutor, Kim Joo-young. Joo-young only accepts two pupils a year but assures a 100% success rate to the students she takes on. The rest of the cast is composed of other families living in the condominium complex, including the Cha family, who expects both of their twin sons to achieve high test scores at the behest of their father, a wealthy law professor. The Woo family, who already have high expectations of their middle-school son, and the Hwang family, newcomers to the *SKY Castle* complex, are among the competing parents in the game of university admissions.

*Emily: SKY Castle* revolves around the hyper-competitive world of high school education, but the drama couldn't exist without real-world inspiration. Each family wants their children to enter SNU's medical school, and this burden is placed on the shoulders of each household's mother, each of whom micromanages their children's extracurricular activities, study time, and social events to ensure the best chance of success. Mrs Park has the same approach in *Parasite*.

South Korea is one of the most highly educated countries in the world. Among Organisation for Economic Co-operation and Development (OECD) countries, Korea has the highest proportion of citizens who have attained tertiary education, and a relatively low proportion of the population participates in vocational or trade school.[1] This enthusiasm for education has been dubbed 'education fever'. Korean parents fervently try to get their children into the best middle schools, which gives them a chance of entering a prestigious high school, which will hopefully lead to an elite university education; and even the youngest students aren't spared from the pressure. Korea has the highest school enrolment rate for 3-year-olds of any OECD country. While this national passion for education has propelled Korea into economic prosperity in a relatively short span, it has also been criticised for being overly rigid and all-consuming, often at the expense of students' wellbeing.

## University exam

Of all the moments in a young Korean student's life, almost none hold as much weight as the university entrance exam, called *suneung* (수능), which is an abbreviation of *daehaksuhangneungnyeoksiheom* (대학수학능력시험) 'college scholastic ability test'. Test results determine which university applicants can enter. Since the inception of the Ministry of Education in South Korea, the college entrance exam, and college entrance requirements, have been through numerous changes and iterations.

However, the standardised university entrance exam has always been an essential component to achieving admission to a top university. The *suneung* is administered only once a year, meaning that if a student wishes to retake the test, they must wait until the next year's exam period. Many students who do not achieve their desired score on their first attempt spend the next year, or several years, studying in the hopes of getting a better result instead of enrolling in a lower-ranked university or entering the job market.[2]

The *suneung* exam, and the versions that came before it, are rooted in the civil servant exam administered during the Goryeo and Joseon dynasties. Passing the civil servant examination was an important goal for nearly every young, upper-class man of the era. Success in these examinations could secure a lofty government position for any man who passed, which in turn helped secure success and power for their future sons. Like its successor, the civil service exam was administered only infrequently, and many men spent years studying and preparing for the civic exam.

College entrance exams are a central part of the Korean education system, and schools, private academies, and tutors all focus on preparing students for this all-important final test. This has led to criticism both at home and abroad, with teachers and schools accused of 'teaching to the test', and placing too strong a focus on exam scores, as opposed to curating a well-rounded curriculum.

There are casualties of this system to support this criticism too. An all-too-common narrative of one such casualty is presented in *SKY Castle* (2018) in the first episode, when a mother whose son was just admitted to the prestigious SNU medical school commits suicide days after his admission. It is later revealed that in an act of rebellion, her son had declined his acceptance and run away with his lower-class girlfriend, his form of revenge for a life where studying and grades took precedence over everything else.

Long school days and the ever-present pressure of the university entrance exam has contributed to high levels of stress for Korean students. Korean students get the least amount of sleep of students from any other OECD country and spend the most hours studying.[3] In the drama, students are shown fighting with their parents and breaking down over the intense pressure to perform academically. Students from all backgrounds, rich or poor, young or old, are shown struggling to keep up with expectations and the competitive nature of Korean school life.

Not only do Korean students study long hours for an all-important exam, but it is not uncommon for schools to encourage students to compete among themselves by publicly posting class ranking or exam scores. A scene in *SKY Castle* (2018) shows two young students looking up at a bulletin board, with the top two scorers' pictures posted for the entire school to see. These public displays of achievement are not uncommon and fuel the competitive nature of students and parents, both in the drama and in real life.

This all can take a toll on Korean students. South Korea has a higher-than-average suicide rate among grade students and college students, a fact which many attribute to the stressful school environment. While *SKY Castle* does not depict teen suicide due to stress, a recent high school graduate, Young-jae, runs away from home to escape the constant pressure, which he fears will only continue when he enters SNU. He shouts that living like this, with endless studying and no free time, is "like living in hell". His mother, distraught that her son has abandoned not only his hard-won admission, but also his family, commits suicide in the first episode.

In the fervour to achieve perfect exam results, many students and their parents turn to private cram schools, or *hagwons* (학원), which provide after-school classes. These classes may focus on specific subjects, test prep, or extracurriculars the student may not learn in their school. *Hagwons* were banned in 1955 by then-president Syngman Rhee, under the premise that it gave unfair access to children of wealthy parents who could afford the academies' fees. The institution of the *suneung* was intended to create an egalitarian meritocracy, where any student could achieve collegiate success if they scored high on this standardised exam. Rhee felt that *hagwons* undermined those egalitarian ideals; however, this did not stop parents from seeking out tutors and under-the-table advantages for their children. The ban was overturned in the 1990s. Now, children from all backgrounds regularly attend *hagwons* for the sake of revision, for topic specialisation, or to learn a subject not typically taught in schools. Elite and prestigious *hagwons* can also be found, particularly in the wealthy neighbourhoods of Seoul. These *hagwons* boast the admission rates of their students to top universities.

## English

Returning to *Parasite*, the article that Mr Park has framed on his wall is written in English and talks of his success in New York in the US. The Parks' also follow the convention of using English and education abroad as social capital. They use English sentences, even to each other when there is no need. When they speak to staff, sometimes they use colloquial English phrases at random, which may even be confusing for Koreans. Mrs Park at one point says "I am deadly serious" to Ki-jung, when Ki-jung asks if she is sure about hiring Mr Kim as a driver. There is no need to use the word 'deadly', and it feels unnatural and silly. However, status is imperatively important to the Park family, and so they use the phrases they know to show it.

Jieun:  *Parasite* plays on this kind of behaviour in Korean society, and how ridiculous it is. English is an asset, and that is precisely how the Park family uses it; for there is no other linguistic value. It is more like a part of their costume that they put on for Korean society – to show them who they are.

Loli:  Famously, Ki-jung sings, "Jessica, only child, Illinois, Chicago, Classmate Kim Jin-mo, he's your cousin" with Ki-woo to memorise her false identity before entering the Park household for her interview. Importantly, the jingle highlights how she uses a foreign university and English language as a symbol of her status. This is invisible to non-Korean viewers.

The 6-second 'Jessica Jingle', as it is known online, also became an element of *K-*, when it went viral.[4] It is actually based on a famous Korean children's song called *Dokdo Is Our Land*, and its tune is used commonly by Korean students to memorise information. However, this is not how it is interpreted by non-Koreans; for viewers around the globe the jingle became a fun element of popular culture. *Parasite*'s American distributor even made the jingle available to download as a ringtone. There have since been many variations of the 'Jessica Jingle'.

*Emily:* While a spot at one of Korea's top universities is an important step to a lucrative career, some aspects of education are considered extra important. Certain academic achievements are associated with affluence and high social status. Namely, speaking English and studying abroad (in an Anglophone country) are seen as status symbols.

The use of English to convey status is not uncommon in Korean media, and that's exactly what we see in *Parasite*, and in the conversations of the mothers living in the *SKY Castle* condominium. These women pepper their conversations with English words. Similarly, English names are also used often, such as in *Parasite* when the Park family call Ki-jung 'Jessica' and Ki-woo 'Kevin'.

Studying abroad, or attending university abroad is often considered a symbol of high status, in part because university tuition in countries like the US and the UK is typically much higher than tuition for Korean universities. Paying for years of international tuition, or even just one semester, is out of reach for many families. Additionally, Korean students learn English from a young age but may or may not reach a high level of proficiency. Hiring a private tutor to teach English is also an extra expense, especially if one plans to hire a native speaker, typically expats living in Korea. The fervent desire to ensure English fluency has led to a phenomenon called "wild goose fathers" or "wild goose families", in which the father (or sometimes both parents) stays in Korea while sending their children to live abroad. Some families do it to "spare their children" from the pressure-cooker environment of Korean schools, and others see it as a necessary sacrifice to make English learning the centre of their children's education.[5]

There are no "goose fathers" in *SKY Castle*, but the Cha family has succeeded in sending their eldest daughter to Harvard, which earns them the admiration of other parents living in the condominium complex and gives the father a sense of authority compared to other families. Not only is Harvard significantly more expensive than any Korean university, the combination of English skills and test scores required for admission make it a source of pride for the entire Cha household.

*Jieun:* Interestingly, at the same time as English and American Ivy league education is so desirable and valued in Korean society, there is also a negative association surrounding American culture. We are very grateful for the help we received from the US during the Korean war. They gave Korea a lot of food, which made a huge difference, but there was also abuse and other unsettling issues which have remained.

Loli:   This dichotomy is particularly interesting if we consider how different representations of intercultural encounters between Korea and the West on-screen are interpreted – the K- that arises from it and the Korean-ness, the visible and invisible.

## Parental capital

In *SKY Castle*, the suicide committed by a mother whose son has rejected his place in elite society shows that academic achievement reflects on not only the student but the entire family. In the first episode, a lavish dinner party is thrown for Young-jae's mother, congratulating *her* on her success in getting her son admitted to the nation's top medical school. She is lauded for her hard work and dedication. Her son, on the other hand, barely makes an appearance at the party.

Confucian values play a major role in this since academic success is a display of filial piety. In the Joseon dynasty, performing well on the civil service exam increased the status of the entire family. In modern Korea, students who study hard and enter elite universities are praised for making their parents proud, and the parents are in turn praised for raising such a studious and disciplined child.

The theme of tying family status to the academic success of one's children is present throughout the drama. Young-jae's mother commits suicide upon learning of her son's rejection. Seo-jin is obsessed with making her daughter, Ye-seo, a student of SNU's medical school, to have three generations of doctors in the family and earn the respect of her mother-in-law. Seo-jin feels that her daughter's success will redeem her of her own past, mired in poverty. The patriarch of the Cha family, Min-hyuk, is obsessed over his twin sons' test prep. He feels that they will be able to reach 'the top of the pyramid' by becoming important politicians, a title he himself was unable to attain. When Min-hyuk learns that his eldest daughter lied about her admission to Harvard, he disowns her entirely.

Although pressure on Korean students to succeed can come from teachers or school systems, much of it can come from their families. Confucianism has always placed a strong value on education, as both a display of moral character and a tool for socio-economic gain.[6] Due to this, the mothers of *SKY Castle* take on their children's education as a full-time job. In one scene, for instance, tutor Kim Joo-yeong dismisses a prospective client for being a working mother, saying she will not have the time to dedicate herself to her child's academic needs. This belief is not uncommon in Korean society, stating that parents, especially mothers, need to be fully available to manage their children and households. Fathers in *SKY Castle* are invested in their child's success but are shown as important members of hospitals and universities, and the duties of coordinating school life fall to the mother of their respective families. While women in Korea are just as likely as men to receive a tertiary education, they are significantly less likely to participate in the work-force, especially after marriage.[7] In *SKY Castle*, one prospective client is praised for discontinuing her PhD thesis so that she could focus on raising her children. The education of children falls largely to the mother in all levels of Korean society, although recent years have shown an increase in women joining and staying in the workforce.

## College coordinator

One of the central characters of *SKY Castle* is Kim Joo-young, a highly sought-after college coordinator. In other words, Joo-young serves as not only a tutor, but as a mentor who reorganises her pupils' workspaces for ultimate concentration potential, schedules all their extracurricular activities, and ensures success in student body elections.

*Emily:* Joo-young uses less than scrupulous efforts to guarantee her students' academic success, but do these all-powerful college coordinators really exist?

In *SKY Castle*, Joo-young's services are only available to VVIPs, the ultra-wealthy clients of Korea's top banks. Matches to coordinators are conducted in secret meetings that require private invitation. Surprisingly, this may be entirely accurate. Producers of the show say that the drama was created "based on real events with meticulous research". In an interview with the *JoongAng Ilbo* newspaper, Lee Man-gi, a veteran tutor and education director, says that these VVIP meetings and lectures are not a work of fiction – and the more famous the client, the more secretive the meetings. These kinds of intensive university coordinators are illegal, and private tutors are not allowed to make over ₩300,000 an hour (approx. £190) but these exclusive coordinators may be paid much, much more in backroom deals. According to Lee, "70% of what is shown in the drama is accurate".[8] Luxury car dealerships, banks, and other industries may hold lectures on the *suneung* exam for wealthy but anxious parents. Coordinators choose which clubs that students can join and may even write parts (or all) of their university applications. The extent of Joo-young's role may be slightly exaggerated, but these sorts of undercover operations give affluent families an extra edge when it comes to their child's future.

The true force of Joo-young power is shown when Ha Seo-jin attempts to re-hire Joo-young, having previously fired her as a coordinator for Ye-seo. Although Joo-young is technically Seo-jin's client, as it is Seo-jin who is paying her, Joo-young is the one who holds all of the power in the situation. Seo-jin attempts to bribe her with expensive gifts and literal gold bars but eventually resorts to begging and pleading. Seo-jin eventually gets down on hands and knees and does a deep bow before Joo-young. This form of prostration is done by people in a low position to their superior. It is often performed in front of grandparents during holidays such as New Year's Day as a sign of respect, or as an act of apology for a grave error.

CEOs or celebrities are known to publicly prostrate themselves after being caught in a scandal. No matter its reason, this bow, or *jeol*, is a sign of humility and deference. The fact that Seo-jin is performing this *jeol* to Joo-young indicates that she considers herself lower than the coordinator. Although Joo-young is a paid consultant, Seo-jin believes her to be the key to her daughter's future.

## Notes

1 Seth, M. J. 2002. *Education Fever: Society, Politics, and the Pursuit of Schooling in South Korea* (Ser. Hawai'i Studies on Korea). Hawai'i: University of Hawai'i Press and Center for Korean Studies.
2 Seth, M. J. 2002. *Education Fever: Society, Politics, and the Pursuit of Schooling in South Korea* (Ser. Hawai'i studies on Korea). Hawai'i: University of Hawai'i Press and Center for Korean Studies.
3 OECD. 2021. "Korea – Education GPS – OECD." *OECD*. Retrieved October 22, 2021, from https://gpseducation.oecd.org/CountryProfile?primaryCountry=KOR&treshold=10&topic=EO
4 Yonhap. 2019. "Doorbell Song from 'Parasite' Hits Internet." *The Korea Herald*. www.koreaherald.com/view.php?ud=20191118000515
5 Kang, J. K. 2012, May 17. "S. Korean 'Goose Fathers' So Lonely They Keep Flies." *Reuters*. Retrieved November 20, 2021, from www.reuters.com/article/us-korea-goosefathers/s-korean-goose-fathers-so-lonely-they-keep-flies-idUSBRE84G0IZ20120517
6 Lee, J.-K. 2006. "Educational Fever and South Korean Higher Education." *Revista Electrónica De Investigación Educativa*, 8(1), pp. 1–14.
7 Cooke, F. L. 2010. "Women's Participation in Employment in Asia: A Comparative Analysis of China, India, Japan, and South Korea." *International Journal of Human Resource Management*, 21(12), pp. 2249–2270. https://doi.org/10.1080/09585192.2010.509627
8 Yoon, S.-Man. 2018, December 22. "아파트 한 채 값 'SKY캐슬'의 입시 코디···70%는 진실." 중앙일보. Retrieved November 20, 2021, from www.joongang.co.kr/article/23231601#home

# 5

# MR SUNSHINE

*Miseuteo Seonshaein* (미스터 선샤인) 'Mr Sunshine' (2018) is a historical drama that takes place at the end of the Joseon dynasty, between the years 1871 and 1907. The story follows a Korean American marine, Eugene Choi, who returns to Hanseong (modern-day Seoul) as part of a diplomatic mission with the US legation. There he meets Lady Ae-sin, a young noblewoman who moonlights as a member of the Righteous Army, a volunteer army who fought against Japanese influence in the hopes of maintaining Joseon's sovereignty and independence. Eventually, a romance blossoms between Eugene and Ae-sin, who is arranged to be married to a young nobleman.

With the romance between Eugene and Lady Ae-sin in the foreground, *Mr Sunshine* references many real-world events such as the US expedition to Korea, and the subsequent Battle of Ganghwa, as well as the Korea Treaty of 1905, and Battle of Namdaemun. Many characters in *Mr Sunshine* are depictions of actual people as well, such as Emperor Gojong, Ito Hirobumi, Japan's first Prime Minister, and Hayashi Gonsuke, Korean diplomat to Korea from Japan.

At its core, *Mr Sunshine* is about the rapid political and cultural changes happening in Joseon at the turn of the century – the people who bought and sold Joseon to foreign powers, and those who gave their lives to defend it. The drama has been both praised and criticised for being pro- or anti-Korea, depending on who you ask.[1] However, regardless of any underlying views by the series' showrunners, *Mr Sunshine* reveals many aspects of Korean culture.

### Suit, kimono, or *hanbok*?

*Mr Sunshine* takes place at a time when the Joseon dynasty was slowly emerging from a long period of isolationism. Joseon was nicknamed "the Hermit

DOI: 10.4324/9781003203230-5

Kingdom"; even after China and Japan were forcibly opened to outside trade by US "gunboat diplomacy", the Joseon maintained its isolation. Repeated efforts by the US to open Joseon to trade eventually led to an incident in which Korean civilians attacked and destroyed SS *General Sherman*, a US merchant ship. The ship's disappearance caused the launch of the US expedition to Korea, which culminated with the Battle of Ganghwa, where Korean soldiers fought with the American Navy. In *Mr Sunshine*, the Battle of Ganghwa is a major focus of the early episodes and sets the scene for the chaotic future that is about to befall the Joseon dynasty.

*Emily:* We see this in episode 1 of *Mr Sunshine*, which has a long scene depicting the Battle of Ganghwa. This battle was a turning point when it came to ending Joseon's isolationism. The American Navy, with stronger artillery and more troops, defeated the Korean forces and captured most of the survivors. Even though Korea was defeated, the government in Seoul refused to sign a treaty or negotiate trade with the US.

In Korean, the Battle of Ganghwa is called *Shinmiyangyo* (신미양요), which literally translates to "Western Disturbance in the Year of Shinmi", and in *Mr Sunshine*, it is depicted as a battle in which Koreans are fighting fiercely and without fear against an enemy who greatly overpowered them in both numbers and technology. This is a view backed up by historical records.[2]

The rapid cultural change during this period of Korean history is evident in the costumes, scenery, and language of *Mr Sunshine*. Storefront signage can be seen in Korean, Japanese, and English. Similarly, characters frequently switch between Korean, Japanese, and English in their dialogue. Characters might be seen in *hanbok*, kimono, or popular Western fashions. These costume choices help the audience

**FIGURE 5.1** Clothing reflects one's political stance, in *Mr Sunshine*.

understand each character's loyalties and motivations. Are they traditional or modern? Are they pro-American or pro-Japanese? Are they loyal to Joseon, or do they support the expansion of foreign powers on the Korean peninsula?

Other characters, such as Kim Hui-seong, use clothing to not only show cultural loyalties but also flaunt their affluence. In this period, the Western suit was a symbol of wealth. Kim Hui-seong, a rich nobleman who has studied abroad, is shown at tailor's shops receiving fine suits that reflect European fashions. For Hui-seong, suits establish him not only as a well-off nobleman but also as a man of the world. Other wealthy *yangban*, such as the emperor's advisers, wear elaborate *hanbok*. In later episodes, the division of loyalty is shown even more clearly through clothing: the ministers who remain loyal to the emperor dress in traditional *hanbok*, while those who are "willing to sell their country to the highest bidder" wear Western clothing, indicating their true motivations.

*Jieun:* Once, when I showed my children a picture book with characters wearing Western and others wearing traditional Korean clothes, my children thought that those wearing Western clothing were rich and those in traditional clothing were poor.

Western suits are not the only foreign clothing that indicates personal interests in *Mr Sunshine*. The character Gu Dong-mae, a Korean butcher-turned-Japanese *yakuza* head, was born as the son of a butcher. At this time, butchers were considered *baekjeong*, low-born members of society on a similar level to slaves. Although butchers (and other members of this caste, such as wicker-makers) were always considered low-born through the Joseon dynasty, contempt for *baekjeong* grew considerably stronger during the late Joseon period.[3] Unlike slaves, butchers did not have to inherit their occupation from their parents, but due to the intense discrimination faced by *baekjeong*, children of butchers rarely had many options besides taking up their parents' trade.

Due to the discrimination and violence that Gu endured as a child of the *baekjeong* caste, he flees to Japan where he joins the Mushin Society – a mercenary *yakuza* group. He rises to the top of the gang and becomes an influential part of the pro-Japanese movement in the Joseon. When Gu returns to Joseon after becoming integrated into the Japanese *yakuza*, he wields more power and influence than he could have dreamed of had he remained in his homeland.

*Yakuza* in the media are often depicted as high-flying, wealthy criminals. In *Mr Sunshine*, for instance, the Mushin Society has money and power on par with nobles like the character. Historically, however, the *yakuza* have been composed of members of the *burakumin* class (the Japanese equivalent of *baekjeong*) and social outcasts. In Japan, the *yakuza* and *burakumin* are tightly linked, and nowadays it is estimated that anywhere between 30% and 70% of *yakuza* members are from *burakumin* bloodlines.[4] Therefore, it's not unreasonable to conceive that even though Gu is a butcher's son, and a Joseon man at that, he could rise to become a leader in an influential *yakuza* organisation.

Gu Dong-mae is shown wearing a kimono throughout the entirety of the drama, showing his rejection of his home country and disregard for the fate of Joseon. Gu is a hired sword, and willing to fight for or against Joseon depending on who is paying him. More than loyalty to Japan itself, Gu displays his dedication to the Japanese crime organisation which took him in and who he considers as family.

Finally, we have the Korean traditional dress, *hanbok*. People from all social classes are seen wearing *hanbok* throughout the drama. *Yangban*, like Lady Ae-sin, are seen in elaborate and colourful *hanbok*, while her servants wear simple *hanbok* in muted colours. Although Lady Ae-sin comes from considerable wealth, she does not regularly wear Western dress like Hui-seong. Ae-sin is shown to be a member of the Righteous Army and regularly puts herself in danger to fight for Joseon's sovereignty against foreign adversaries. Through her action and her clothing, she is shown to be loyal to Joseon through and through. The only time Ae-sin is seen in Western dress is when she is hiding her identity to perform clandestine operations with the Righteous Army. During training for the Righteous Army, Ae-sin wears a simple, male *hanbok* that resembles the *hanbok* worn by the working class.

*Jieun:* A little further trivia on the word *hanbok*: the meaning and origin of the word '*han*', which we come across in '*han-bok*' and '*han-geul*', is still unknown, even though it repeatedly appears in some key Korean objects, such as Korean traditional costume and the Korean alphabet. For instance, nobody knows who first used the term '*hangeul*', despite the significance of the writing system's invention. The Chinese use the word *han* to describe their national identity, which mystifies me further over '*han*' when used in Korean, because it also seems to represent Korean-ness too. Joo-sik Young argues that the Korean word '*han*' means 'big and great' – so *hangeul* was chosen to mean 'big and great Korean alphabet'.

### *Jangot*, palanquins, and neo-Confucian womanhood

The *hanbok* worn by Lady Ae-sin is slightly different from the one worn by lower-class women in Joseon. Viewers will likely have noticed that whenever Ae-sin is out in public, she wears cape-like headwear that shields her face.

*Loli:* When women did leave the home, regardless of who they were meeting or what they were doing, they would avoid showing their face in public to appear virtuous, especially *yangban* women.

*Emily:* Noblewomen typically travelled in a palanquin, which shielded them from public view. When they were outside of the palanquin, they wore *jangot* (장옷), which was a type of head covering that resembled a long coat, however, where you might expect the coat to sit on the shoulders and hang down, instead it hung down from the head.

FIGURE 5.2    Lady Ae-sin wearing the *jangot*, in *Mr Sunshine*.

The *jangot* was a symbol of modesty, and it was expected that women of most social classes would wear some sort of headwear when leaving the house. As a noblewoman, Lady Ae-sin is even further guarded from the public. Whenever she steps outside her home, she is carried in a palanquin that prevents anyone from seeing her.

During the Joseon dynasty, Korea's development of neo-Confucianism influenced nearly every aspect of a woman's life. From birth, to marriage, to death, neo-Confucian ideals strictly regulated what sort of behaviour was considered acceptable for women, at every social level. For *yangban* women especially, the shift to a more patrilineal system was especially restrictive.

It had not always been so, though. Prior to the Joseon era, a husband typically moved in with his wife's family after marriage, and women had the right to equal inheritance alongside their brothers. During the Joseon dynasty, customs were changed so that a woman instead moved out of her family home and in with her in-laws, and the amount of inheritance a woman was allowed to receive was drastically decreased. Additionally, before the Joseon period, the role of carrying out ancestral rites was distributed between all descendants, both female and male. At the same time women lost the right to equal inheritance, they also lost the right to perform ancestral rites. This in turn increased the pressure on couples to produce a son, to have a male heir who could perform ancestral rites for them after their death.[5]

In the *yangban* class, a man could only have one official wife but frequently had many concubines too. If a man's official wife failed to bear a son, the male child of a concubine could then become the inheritor of his father's land and slaves and perform ancestral rites for the family.

*Emily:* Lady Ae-sin's cousin, Go Ae-soon, is the official wife of a *yangban* man. However, Ae-soon seems to be unable to have a child and so she raises a concubine's son as her own, all the while on the receiving end of abuse from her husband due to her infertility. *Yangban* wives during this period probably felt constant pressure to produce a male heir, all the while afraid that they would fall out of favour with their husband or in-laws.

When it came to marriage, *yangban* women were not given much say in *who* they married either. From the beginning of *Mr Sunshine*, Lady Ae-sin is betrothed to Kim Hui-seong, whom she has never met. They have been engaged for 10 years, an arrangement made by their parents. At this time, the youngest age men and women could get married was 14 and 15 years, respectively. However, to create favourable connections with other influential families, parents often betrothed their son or daughter long before they even reach this already young age.

*Emily:* The marriage between Ae-sin and Hui-seong is not a marriage of love but instead a plan to join two of Joseon's most powerful families.

With so much importance placed on marriage and childbearing, one of the most important virtues a Joseon woman was expected to have was chastity. Just as a good and loyal subject was said to only serve one king, a good and virtuous wife should only serve one husband. Joseon women were even forbidden to remarry if their husband died. Even married couples practically never interacted with each other outside of the marital bedchamber, let alone a man and woman meeting without being married.

*Emily:* Lady Ae-sin and Eugene take great pains to only meet in secret, as any mention of Lady Ae-sin meeting a man in private (let alone an American) could ruin her reputation, and by extension her family's reputation too.

Women resided in their own quarters, called *anchae*, which were separated from the men's living quarters, or *sarangchae*. Lady Ae-sin is frequently seen reading, sleeping, and living in a small one-room building, which is not connected to any other rooms in the estate. This is likely her own private chamber within the *anchae*, while the men of the family live in buildings elsewhere on the property. Unlike Western-style manor homes in which men, women, and servants might live in distinct quarters within one large house, *yangban* estates typically consisted of multiple buildings which may or may not be joined by a hallway.

*Emily:* Even when they went out with their husbands, women were required to walk several steps behind them.
*Jieun:* This is because married couples were expected to appear as if they were strangers in public. The act of living, eating, and walking separately was a key aspect of the Confucian philosophical concept of *bubuyubyeol* (부부유별) husband and wife have order, which dictates that the duties and responsibilities of men and women are different and separate.

## Hair

Aside from clothing, hair was also a strong indicator of whether one identified as a person of Joseon or not. Korean men and women would not cut their hair during their lifetime, as a Confucian cultural practice that was intrinsically linked to their identity and respect of oneself and one's family. Hair was considered a gift from one's parents. In the teachings of Confucius, it was said that "The human body, hair, and flesh are inherited from parents. Dare not to damage is the beginning of filial piety."[6] Confucian scholars and the public protested at the time, arguing, "Even if you cut your hands and feet, you can't cut your hair." Men would tie their long hair in a topknot, which was considered a basic sign of respectability and unthinkable not to do so, while women would wear their hair in plaited styles.

A few important haircuts happen in *Mr Sunshine*. The first is when Eugene, having travelled secretly to America, is taunted for his long, plaited hair. After witnessing a parade of marines pass by, he takes a knife and begins to cut off his long hair and vows to assimilate into American society. As a young boy raised in Confucian society, the act of cutting his hair severs him from his Korean identity.

*Emily:* Specifically, Eugene is inspired to join the US Marines after he sees a young black marine alongside white soldiers. Coming from an ethnically homogenous society to an ethnically heterogeneous one, the sight of the two marines of different races is what leads him to believe that he can "become an American." Historically, immigrants from Korea did serve in the US military during this period, and there is record of Korean American soldiers fighting in the Spanish-American War of 1898.

FIGURE 5.3   Sa-hong lets down his hair as an act of protest against the Japanese influence in Joseon Korea, in *Mr Sunshine*. His hair is a symbol of defiance and desperation.

Men of all social classes always kept their hair tied up in topknots, and the sight of one's untied hair was considered intensely intimate and inappropriate for public spaces. In episode 17 of *Mr Sunshine*, Ae-sin's grandfather, a close adviser to the emperor, leads a protest begging the emperor to fight back against Japanese interference in Joseon. The elderly Sa-hong is supported by a throng of young aristocratic scholars, all of whom wait in front of the palace with their long hair untied from their topknot. This act, of letting their hair down, is a strong sign of resistance. It shows that the educated and wealthy *yangban* are willing to not only protest social norms but commit an act that is otherwise humiliating. The sight of dozens of respected ministers with their hair out of its customary topknot is sure to draw public attention to their request.

In the next episode, we see a haircut not done by choice, but by force. The *yakuza* leader, Gu Dong-mae, approaches Lady Ae-sin underneath a bridge, and in one surprise motion cuts off her long plait. This act shocks all the passers-by, and Lady Ae-sin is quickly taken away. To have one's haircut is already seen as shameful in Confucian society, but Lady Ae-sin was attacked by a member of the lower classes, adding further insult to the already humiliating ordeal. At a deeper level, Gu Dong-mae has begun the process of Lady Ae-sin's Westernisation. By this point in the series, Joseon is on the brink of complete occupation by Japanese forces, and more and more characters are seen sporting Japanese- or Western-style dress and hairstyles. Lady Ae-sin's grandfather comforts her after the incident by saying that more and more people are cutting their hair, hinting at the increasingly changing norms and customs.

During the Japanese occupation, Koreans were forced to abandon their traditions and heritage. One of the ways in which Koreans were required to assimilate was by cutting their hair. While cutting one's hair was still considered disrespectful to one's family, many Koreans did not have a choice after the annexation. Perhaps most notably, even the emperor of Joseon is seen with short hair towards the end of the series. By this point, the emperor is merely a figurehead, and he possesses no power or influence over the foreign governments that have entered Korea.

**FIGURE 5.4**  Gu surprises Ae-sin by cutting her hair, in *Mr Sunshine*.

Emperor Gojong did indeed cut his hair and later abdicated the throne. An edict made in 1895 required all Korean men to cut their topknots, and the emperor was not exempt. Sources say that a Japanese barber was the one to cut Emperor Gojong's hair, since all Korean barbers refused to perform such a disrespectful act against the monarch.

*Emily:* The act of putting one's hair up in a topknot was considered a symbol of transitioning from boy to man in Joseon society. Regardless of age, once a young boy had hair long enough to be put in a topknot, he was given the respect of an adult. The haircuts enforced during Japanese occupation were a tactic to emasculate Korean men and assert power over the Joseon government.

## Newspapers

*Mr Sunshine* is immediately recognisable to both Korean and foreign viewers as a historical drama. The costumes, the scenery, and the way characters conduct themselves evoke a turn-of-the-century feeling. However, non-Korean viewers may not pick up immediately on another giveaway of the drama's epoch: the language.

Even novice speakers will likely notice that the language spoken in *Mr Sunshine* doesn't sound like the Korean they've studied. During this period, the Korean language was in a stage now known as *Early Modern Korean*, as opposed to Modern Korean, which is the type of Korean spoken nowadays. Just as Joseon's culture and society were undergoing a period of change, so too was their language. Prior to opening trade with Western countries, the Korean language had very few loan words from European languages. Even native Korean speakers may not recognise some of the historical terms used in *Mr Sunshine*, which is why the drama sometimes uses subtitles to provide the Modern Korean translation of a now non-operational word.

Although the native Korean writing system, *hangeul*, had been invented by King Sejong in 1443, it still was not in wide use by the turn of the 20th century. Aristocrats preferred to write in *hanja*, or Chinese characters, and many members of the lower classes did not have access to written texts. This was changing during the end of the Joseon dynasty. Emperor Gojong instituted sweeping reforms in the 1890s that required official documents to be written in *hangeul*. Prior to this, documents were written in *hangeul* only occasionally.

Different characters are seen interacting with *hangeul* and *hanja* throughout the series, and each interaction gives glimpses into their own daily lives and background. In the first episode, Ae-sin receives newspapers smuggled in by a jewellery merchant.

Although it would be inappropriate for an aristocratic lady to be reading a newspaper, Lady Ae-sin pays the merchant to receive news of daily ongoing events in Hanseong, in addition to reading other socially acceptable texts. As a woman from a wealthy family, Ae-sin would have had access to learning both *hangeul* and *hanja*. Prior to its widespread use, *hangeul* was regarded as a woman's script, and upper-class women kept diaries written in *hangeul*.[7]

Even after the Gabo reform made *hangeul* more accessible to lower classes, it didn't mean that everyone had access to learning it. In the same episode, two bounty hunters are seen puzzling over a newspaper written in *hangeul*. At the time, it was also common to see documents in mixed script, with both *hangeul* and *hanja*. This method of writing was common all the way into the 20th century, and some Korean language newspapers still use *hanja* to specify words.

Just because *hangeul* was becoming more widely used does not mean that *hanja* was being replaced entirely. Even when King Sejong invented *hangeul* in 1443, many aristocrats pushed back against using the vernacular script. Aristocrats benefited greatly from being the only literate members of society, and replacing Chinese script with a native one caused fears that Joseon would anger China. As such, many if not all scholars continued to use *hanja* well into the 20th century. When Sa-hong writes his plea to Emperor Gojong, he does not do so in *hangeul* but in *hanja*.

Although *hangeul* is now a great source of pride for Korea, it was not always that way. However, when Japan annexed Korea, Japanese authorities banned the use of *hangeul* altogether. Using *hangeul* was a symbol of resistance to Japanese culture, signifying pride in Korean heritage.

*Emily:* As the situation in Joseon becomes more dire, Hui-seong takes it upon himself to use his wealth to open an independent newspaper.

Even the *hangeul* written in *Mr Sunshine* looks different to what viewers may be used to today. At this time, the Korean language, both spoken and written, was in a period of transition. Lady Ae-sin frequently uses the *haoche* (하오체) speech style, a semi-formal or 'middle' speech style that is rarely used in Modern Korean. In historical dramas, the use of *haoche* in dialogue adds to a feeling of antiquity and distinguishes the *yangban* class from commoners. Lady Ae-sin frequently uses the *haoche* speech style when speaking to Eugene, servants, or anyone who is at or below her noble rank. She can be heard saying *mianhao* (미안하오), instead of *mianhae* (미안해) or *mianhaeyo* (미안해요) 'I'm sorry', either of which are more common in the language of the modern era. *Haoche*, when used nowadays, typically sounds awkward and old-fashioned. It is now usually only found on signage or advertisements. The *haoche* style is also seen in some writing on-screen in *Mr Sunshine*, such as when Lady Ae-sin writes Eugene notes in this style.

*Emily:* This is one of my favourite scenes in *Mr Sunshine*, because it subtly tells us about Eugene's background. Although Eugene is a relatively high-ranking marine, he is completely illiterate in Korean. He can speak Korean fluently but cannot read even Lady Ae-sin's simple message. Eugene obviously moved to the US when he was young, which meant he was distanced from learning Korean writing, but more importantly, he was born a slave. As the child of slaves, he would have had no access to education and no opportunity to learn to read and write. This scene shows not only the difference in Lady Ae-sin and Eugene's cultural upbringings, but the stark difference in their status as people of Joseon. Although Eugene has a successful military career in America, Joseon *yangban* still views him as someone of low birth.

### Jemulpo harbour

One of the most significant locations depicted in *Mr Sunshine* is Jemulpo harbour. Now known as Incheon, the city is a major port city on the west coast of Korea. The port itself was opened in 1883 and was an important thoroughfare in transporting both goods and people through a slowly opening Joseon. Jemulpo is the closest port to Seoul, and as such, many merchants and diplomats relied on this port to enter the country.

In *Mr Sunshine*, the port is shown at strategic times to indicate which foreign powers are entering Joseon. Early in the series, the American ambassador to Joseon is shown entering through Jemulpo harbour, followed closely by American military men. Horace Newton Allen was the first US ambassador to Korea, and he arrived in 1884, just 1 year after the port's opening. The opening on Jemulpo port was also influenced by the Battle of Ganghwa. After Joseon's defeat in the battle with American forces, a treaty was signed in 1882 that eventually led to full-fledged trade.

Jemulpo harbour is shown not only when foreign powers are entering but also when members of the resistance are being smuggled out. Members of the Righteous Army were targeted by pro-Japanese sympathisers, or those who wanted Korea to continue opening to foreign trade. Many characters shown in *Mr Sunshine* are not necessarily against Korea or for Japanese annexation but merely follow the path that they believed would lead to their own monetary gain, regardless of the human cost.

Jemulpo's opening is a symbol of the end of the Hermit Kingdom. Joseon's long period of isolation rapidly shifted to a flurry of trade in and out of Korea, and suddenly people from all over the world were entering Korea, each with different motivations. However, even before *Shinmiyangyo*, and the eventual 1882 treaty that led to full-fledged trade with the US, Joseon was struggling to keep outside influence in check. By the late 19th century, missionaries from Europe and North America had been active in the peninsula for several hundred years. Ambassador Newton originally went to Joseon as a Protestant missionary years before his appointment as ambassador. The fictional character Joseph Stenson, who smuggles Eugene to America, is also a missionary who regularly travels back and forth between the two countries. Joseph is active as a missionary prior to Jemulpo port's opening and is shown transporting Korean goods back to America before trade was officially established between the countries.

## Candy

As the Joseon becomes more and more international, Lady Ae-sin, Gu Dong-mae, and other characters are seen enjoying foreign treats like hard candy, coffee, and French pastries. The opening of a French patisserie and candy stand is a cause for delight among pedestrians on the streets of Hanseong (modern-day Seoul).

*Emily:* Laypeople are seen delighting in the new advancements in technology and luxury goods that are brought to them from other parts of the world. Many could not have anticipated that alongside candies and pastries, foreign trade would eventually bring about the fall of Joseon.

    Traditional Korean desserts are typically sweetened with honey or fruit, as Korea did not have access to cane sugar or other refined sugars. Much of their confections are made from rice or rice flour, such as *tteok* (떡) and *yugwa* (유과), and hard candies would have been a novelty. Korean desserts are often flavoured with sesame, mugwort, red bean, and honey. European flavours, such as chocolate, pistachio, and strawberry, were completely new to the Korean palate. The textures, flavours, and ingredients of foreign cuisine were likely just as exciting for those living in Joseon as shown to be for the characters of *Mr Sunshine*.

*Loli:* In contemporary Korea, there is an array of candy available and many bakeries. Cake culture is very popular. However, older generations still seem more inclined towards traditional Korean tastes when it comes to sweets. This also makes me think of K-ness, in how tradition and contemporaneity, Korean-ness, and Western influence, have all managed to exist simultaneously with neither banished by the other. Often new ways replace old ways and times change, but in Korea, there is an incredible propensity for maintaining culture even when new influences enter the picture.

**FIGURE 5.5** Early experiences of candy and patisserie in the Joseon depicted in *Mr Sunshine*.

Along with new food and drink, the opening of the Hermit Kingdom brought about a wave of new technology. Shortly after Jemulpo harbour began operation, Joseon established its first railroad line. Other scenes in *Mr Sunshine* display the public fascination with electric lights, street cars, and recreational activities such as fencing. The excitement of new products mingled with the apprehension regarding changing social norms is described by Lady Ae-sin when she says, "yesterday seemed like a distant past, today felt unfamiliar, and tomorrow was terrifying. It was a time of turbulence. All of us, each in our own way, were living through the rapidly changing Joseon."[8]

## Notes

1 Dong, Sung-hwa. 2018, July 23. "'Mr. Sunshine' Takes Flack for Leaning to Japan." *The Korea Times.* www.koreatimes.co.kr/www/art/2018/07/688_252682.html
    Oh, Young-jin. 2018, August 2. "Japs Are Bad, Yanks Are Good, Kinda." *The Korea Times.* www.koreatimes.co.kr/www/art/2018/08/688_253136.html
    Park, Jin-hai. 2018, August 21. "'Mr. Sunshine' Embroiled in History Distortion Dispute." *The Korea Times.* www.koreatimes.co.kr/www/art/2018/07/688_252685.html
    Park, Jin-hai. 2018, October 1. "'Mr. Sunshine' Gives New Life to Independence Fighters." *The Korea Times.* www.koreatimes.co.kr/www/culture/2018/10/135_256268.html
2 Schley, Winfield Scott. 1904. "Opening Communication with Korea." Essay. In *Forty-Five Years Under the Flag*, 83–97. New York: D. Appleton.
3 The Organization of Korean Historians, and Michael D. Shin. 2014. *Everyday Life in Joseon-Era Korea: Economy and Society.* Leiden: Brill Academic Publishing.
4 Kaplan, David E., and Alec Dubro. 2003. *Yakuza: The Explosive Account of Japan's Criminal Underworld.* London: Robert Hale.
5 Han, Hee-sook. 2004, December. "Women's Life during the Chosŏn Dynasty." *International Journal of Korean History*, 6.
6 Zi, Zeng. 2008. *Xiao Jing – The Classic of Xiao with English Translation & Commentary* (孝經 英語譯解). http://www.tsoidug.org/Papers/Xiao_Jing_Comment.pdf
7 Kim Haboush, Ja-hyun. 1996. *The Memoirs of Lady Hyegyong: The Autobiographical Writings of a Crown Princess of Eighteenth-Century Korea.* Berkeley and Los Angeles, CA: University of California Press.
8 The last line of episode 1, spoken by Lady Go Ae-sin. 2019. 어제는 멀고, 오늘은 낯설며, 내일은 두려운, 격변의 시간 이었다. 우리 모두는 그렇게, 각자의 방법으로, 격변하는 조선을 지나는 중이었다. Netflix, from the television show Mr. Sunshine, produced by Studio Dragon and Hwa&Dam Pictures.

# 6

# *PACHINKO*

First becoming *K-* during the early interest in K-literature, *Pachinko* (2022) became an instant *New York Times Best Seller*, dubbed one of the "Ten Best Books of 2017". *Pachinko* has since reached a wide audience, with the novel being translated into 27 languages and most recently adapted for the television screen. *Pachinko* season 1 was released by Apple TV+ in 2022 and was widely praised by critics,[1] receiving nomination for an Emmy Award shortly after.[2]

*Pachinko* follows four generations of a Korean immigrant family as they endure poverty, discrimination, loss, joy, and hard-earned success, in the struggle to control their destiny in 20th-century Japan. The story begins in the early 1900s in Korea, after the start of Korea's colonisation by the Japanese, when Sunja discovers that her lover Hansu is married, and her unplanned pregnancy threatens to shame her family. She has no choice but to leave her home, her mother, and everything she knows to protect their reputation, and so when a priest offers to marry her and raise her child as his own, she leaves Korea with him and goes to his home in Japan. The saga of Sunja's family's struggle then begins as generations of family members grapple for acceptance, search for identity, and try to heal the scars of the past.

## Colonisation

The imperial Joseon dynasty had spanned nearly 500 years, beginning in 1392, during which the kingdom had experienced an explosion of cultural and societal change. It was during this dynastic period that the capital was moved to Hanseong (also called Hanyang, and today known as Seoul), *hangeul* was invented and introduced to the people, and neo-Confucianism became the dominant ideology. It was also during this time that the aristocratic class of *yangban* was established, and land and power were redistributed among this class of scholars and noblemen. In 1910,

DOI: 10.4324/9781003203230-6

however, when Korea was annexed by Japan, the Japanese attempted to remove all traces of Korean culture – including language, customs, traditional dress, and food – as part of removing their rights and status. Many Koreans raised during the annexation period couldn't speak Korean. Despite it all, remarkably, Korea managed to maintain its heritage, much of which remains, forming the fundament of the contemporary Korea we know today.

## Scar

Korea and Japan are close geographically. You can get there by aeroplane in an hour. It's like travelling to France from the UK. However, the psychological distance between the two is huge due to the history between the two countries. There is potential for getting along well – there is a recognised cultural overlap, with a structural similarity between the two societies – however, even when living in the same country, there is a huge distance. As a result, second-generation Korean immigrants avoid revealing their *Zainichi* identity, at the risk of discrimination. In fact, the word '*Zainichi*', which is used by the Japanese to describe Korean immigrants in Japan, is discriminating because of the implication, but there has been no other word put forward for describing their nationality.

Subsequently, there is a lot of scar tissue – old and new, explicit and implicit in Japan. *Hansu* has a scar across his eyebrow, acquired during the 1932 earthquake in Tokyo, which was followed by the Massacre of Koreans, who were blamed for the event. These scars defined who he became – his assimilation into the *yakuza*, and renunciation of his Korean identity.

While for Sunja, her scars are shown in how she chooses to protect the younger generations of her family. For instance, when Solomon was young, she kept Solomon and his first love – a Japanese girl – away from each other, after she got him in trouble by asking him to steal something from a shop, to protect him from the discrimination he would experience as a Korean should she get him into trouble again. Years later, having not been able to contact her, his grandmother still encourages him to stay in the US rather than return to Japan, because she believes it is safer. Her scars cause her to interfere; even if it causes her grandson some pain, she believes it will be less than he will endure as a Zainichi in Japan.

Scars are shown to be commonly inflicted on Koreans. For instance, in another scene, an elderly Korean woman of the same generation as Sunja, whose home Solomon attempts to purchase for his company, explains that she can't speak to her own children in Korean because her husband didn't want them to learn it lest they be discriminated against.

Even between friends, there is open discrimination shown between Koreans and Japanese. Solomon carries scars from childhood, inflicted by the words of classmates. In one scene, following his friend's inconsiderate comments, he recalls a time when they were children, and his friend told him that his father said that "Koreans must've been raised by dogs. Why else would they shove their faces in our bowls instead of picking them up like you?" The friend says he doesn't remember saying this, saying his father's words were probably misheard, and blaming it on them being children. Although he admits it is a terrible thing to say, there is a feeling of invalidation and injustice in the way he expresses empathy to Solomon.

There are certain terms used here that strike a sensitive chord with Korean people, beyond being universally insulting. The comparison of Koreans to dogs is made several times throughout the series, showing inherited attitudes and an implicit continuation of colonisation in the supposedly post-colonial period. In Korea the term for 'baby animal', and especially 'dog', are used as a common insult. In Korean '*gae*' means 'dog' and '*saekki*' means 'baby animal', however if you add *gae* (개) or *saeki* (새끼) to another word or use the word in an aggressive context it becomes a profanity. You can even put the two words together in the common swear word '*gae-saekki*', which is commonly translated as something like the word 'bastard'. Thus, use of the word 'dog' can translingually create a similar effect, potentially stimulating an emotional reaction in Korean viewers.

His friend denies knowledge of the incident and condemns the behaviour, but there is a lack of empathy for the seriousness of this behaviour and its effect on Solomon. This scar, like Sunja's, prevents Solomon from feeling safe in Japanese spaces, be they geographical or interpersonal. He can't trust his 'friends'; there's no loyalty or equality with them, no matter how much time they spend together.

There are other kinds of scars too, such as those which Solomon received in the US as an East Asian immigrant. At the same party, he also interacts with his female Japanese colleague about their experience with Americans. They refer to the 'Which Asian' game that Americans play with them, which Solomon calls "a classic". Although this conversation is slightly humorous, it is sarcastic, and the connotation is that these misunderstandings of their nationality are tiresome and offensive.

Then there are those scars caused by rejection from one's own loved ones after assimilating into another cultural environment, making one feel nomadic. Exchanges in interactions take on different meanings when intercultural relations are taken into consideration, such as in another scene at this party, when Solomon's boss asks him "What is your blood type?" when first meeting him. Japanese believe that blood type is an indicator of personality. The question carries the implication that his boss doesn't trust him immediately because he is Korean, and that therefore he is trying to work out what type of 'Korean' he is using the measure of 'blood type'. If this were to occur between Japanese people, the implication would likely be less negative, because the discriminatory nature of the Japanese-Korean social dynamic is removed.

## Pachinko machine

Our first object is *Pachinko's* namesake. The pachinko machine itself is named after the onomatopoeia sound *pacha* or *pachin* (パチン) that the game makes when it is played. Pachinko machines originate from the American children's game "Corinthian Bagatelle", which was popular in the 1920s. The game became popular among adults in Nagoya following World War II, and the first commercial pachinko parlour was opened in Nagoya in 1948, with pachinko becoming big business in Japan ever since. Ironically, gambling is illegal in Japan and yet pachinko has and continues to operate there legally. It does so via a loophole. It is illegal for players to exchange their balls for money directly at the pachinko parlour or to remove the balls from the premises, so the parlours get around this by allowing the exchange of balls for either a ticket that can be exchanged for cash at a separate vendor nearby, or for prizes at the parlour.

The game itself can perhaps be likened to a cross between pinball and a slot machine, though unlike these games, pachinko requires both skill and luck to win and as such can take a lifetime to master. Pachinko players purchase a bucket of balls that are like metal ball bearings. They then launch these balls in the machine and try to direct them into regions of the machine that will trigger a jackpot. If they are successful, the tray of the machine will fill with these balls, which can be exchanged for money or used to continue playing. The skill is in knowing how hard one must launch the ball for it to go down particular pathways that lead to jackpots. How many balls you win each time is down to luck: depending on the pocket your ball lands in, a certain number of balls are triggered; this is unpredictable.

Joining up the dots, viewers might suspect that the show is titled *Pachinko* because it is through the pachinko parlour that the family have been able to thrive in Japan. *Vogue*, for instance, called the name "charming" and referred to this very connection between the title and story.[3] However, there is more to it than that. As with all the objects we present in this book, the pachinko machine has a culture and history surrounding it.

The pachinko machine is a gambling machine, and gambling is one of the industries traditionally under the control of the *yakuza* (Japanese gangsters). Korean immigrants who went to Japan were incredibly limited in what they could do, and for almost all, wealth or security was elusive. In fact, there is an association made between Koreans who had money or social status during the colonisation period and being a traitor, as it implies that they were on good terms with the Japanese government or involved in illegal activities.

*Jieun:* If you have a pachinko parlour, then you will receive good money. But, like Hansu, you will probably be despised by other Koreans. Also, no matter how wealthy you become, you will never be able to remove that stain from your family. The money will be considered 'dirty money'.

*Loli:* Yes, in one of the episodes a businessman is being interviewed on television and he is asked by the reporter about the illicit business that his grandfather has been accused of doing. Even two generations later, the money that has built the family business is considered illegitimate.

Clean money, dirty money. Makes no difference.

FIGURE 6.1    The men talk about clean and dirty money at the pachinko parlour, and the theme continues to be one of the theme strands that are woven together throughout the episodes of *Pachinko*.

It is the association between pachinko and gangs and violence that is an early signifier that Sunja's family received support from Hansu. This is yet to unfold in the television show. This information is the difference between Korean and the *K*-we see in articles like the earlier example from *Vogue*; implicature that will be lost on those without knowledge of Japanese- and Korean-related histories.

Sunja has endured society's disdain, as has her son Mosasu in his knowledge of Hansu's existence and running of the pachinko parlour. Sunja also encourages Mosasu's son, Solomon, to endure the shame he feels about being the son of a pachinko parlour owner. In one scene, shortly after Solomon returns to his family home in Japan having travelled from America, he catches up with his grandmother as they cook together. When she informs him that his father is expanding his business, Solomon's reaction is concerned. Sunja then tells him not to discourage his father.

What Sunja doesn't see is that her grandson is suffering as a third-generation Korean immigrant, because of his Zainichi status and his lifetime association with the pachinko parlour. Solomon has had a different life than Sunja; however, he is faced with experiences rooted in the same bigotry and injustice as she and the Koreans of her day faced. This is often invalidated by older Koreans' attitude that Solomon's generation should feel lucky for what they have, ultimately causing the young to carry guilt for being ungrateful.

The invalidation of Solomon's feelings extends to his interactions with the Japanese too. Even his father's local Japanese friend and Solomon's Japanese childhood friend refer to Solomon's connection to pachinko in a derogatory fashion. It isn't always done purposely to harm him; however, the passivity of this discrimination makes it particularly potent, since for it to get to this stage, where Koreans would simply accept this treatment, they had to be subjected to excessive brutality upon their identity.

In one scene, for instance, Solomon's father's Japanese friend and ex-business partner, Hirota, visits the parlour where he meets Mosasu and Solomon. Hirota congratulates Solomon on his success, since he studied at Harvard University and worked for a large international company in the US. However, he undercuts the compliment by saying that Solomon did well 'for a son of a pachinko man'. In an earlier scene, at Solomon's boss's daughter's wedding, a similar phrase is also used by Solomon's childhood friend, who is also Japanese. In the scene, the two men are talking about how Japan has changed since Solomon went to America. Solomon's friend says that there are "too many people making money too quickly", people who weren't in Japan before. Solomon then replies that "maybe that's what this country needs". To which his friend replies, "like the son of a Pachinko man?", and then insists that he's only joking as only old friends can.

The pachinko machine becomes one of the many tools used to express passive aggression – or what we would like to propose is more specifically in this context 'passive colonialism' – towards Koreans. Looking down on Solomon's father and his father's business by saying "you did well for a pachinko man's son" is very much like saying "You did well for yourself, given that you are Korean", because the reason his father can only be a "pachinko man" is because of the Japanese discrimination. Of course, with colonisation over on paper, the continuation of oppression must take these alternate forms that continue to fail to recognise the Koreans' discrimination and suffering.

## White

White is a colour of cultural significance in Korea. It holds a variety of cultural meanings and is integral to the identity of the Korean people. We discuss a couple of key white objects: rice and *hanbok*.

### White rice

In Korea, rice – *bab* (밥) – is at the centre of every meal. The dinner table itself is called *babsang* (밥상), which translated literally means 'rice table', and the *banchan* (반찬) 'side dishes' that cover the *babsang* – including meat, fish, stews, and soups – are prepared to accompany the rice. Korea's traditional meal consists of four key components: "The first one is *bab* (cooked rice), which provides calories and is the main source of energy."[4] As mentioned in Chapter 3, even when eating another carbohydrate, such as noodles, a bowl of rice is provided too. Food is not considered as a 'meal' without rice. The second is *guk* (국) 'soup', "which allows people to chew and swallow rice, in turn supporting the digestive system".[5] Then *banchan* makes up the third key element, complementing the rice and in doing so, making "the food taste better to support digestion while replenishing the body with nutrition".[6] Finally, *jang* (장) 'sauce' makes up the fourth part, served to stimulate peoples' appetites by enhancing the flavours and increasing the health benefits of present ingredients.[7] Since rice has a comparatively simple taste, all of the other

FIGURE 6.2    The Chinese character 福, which is pronounced *fuì* with a rising tone in Chinese and *bok* in Korean, is engraved on the lid of this Korean rice bowl. The 福 character means 'blessing', and so its placement on the lid of the rice bowl shows the regard in which rice is held in Korea.

components of a Korean meal can be seen as having been developed specifically for a meal in which rice is central.

In the third episode of *Pachinko*, Sunja accompanies Solomon to the home of a fellow Korean ex-pat of the same generation; he has the task of persuading her to sell her land, which is situated in the way of a major development in Tokyo. The woman invites them inside and prepares a meal for them, which upon tasting the rice, Sunja's face undergoes an emotional shift. The other woman recognises Sunja's emotion and understands its origin immediately. "You taste it, don't you?", she says. The rice is grown in Korea, and the taste brings back Sunja's memories of the first and second times that she ever tasted white rice.

Jieun:  Japan and Korea share rice eating, but in those days, it wasn't easy to eat rice.
Loli:   The scene in which Sunja's mother cooks white rice for Sunja, who has never tasted white rice before on the day of her wedding is filled with emotion that transcends Korean interpretation. I connected to this as a mother and a daughter, becoming emotional at the thought of what Koreans must have gone through, and specifically the mother's sacrifice and daughter's loss of her mother. In this respect, I felt that Korean *han* was able to become an element of *K-* under *Pachinko*.

At the crux of these cultural and historical contexts, which are unrelatable and often untranslatable for non-Koreans, is rice. It is the vessel through which we are delivered the emotion of the mother and daughter who are being separated by the situation, and their love for each other. Sunja's mother's desire for her daughter to taste the rice of her own country is an expression of her love because of just how risky and difficult to achieve it is, and how much it means to Sunja to have such an opportunity.

*Jieun:* This scene of Sunja preparing rice for her family demonstrates the continuation of rice and motherhood by Sunja. The rice cooker is frequently featured in the camera frame, and as we are transported between periods this imagery is mirrored again and again. Wherever they go, they eat rice. This marks their identity, among other elements of Korean culture and language. It is a way of continuing their Korean-ness. Sunja's role in this is to feed the family faithfully, and to not stop no matter what situation arises. Even at the hospital, as they visit Solomon's chronically ill ex-girlfriend, Sunja brings rice and side dishes for them to eat.

In episode 3, when Sunja is reminded of the nutty taste of rice grown in Korea, she is transported back to that first time that her mother cooked it on her wedding day. The sequence in which Sunja's mother prepares her daughter's first bowl of white rice gives great focus to the careful preparation of the rice; stressing its meaning and the emotion tied to it in how precisely she treats it, and how she appears to savour the process of preparing it. The scene is poignant in conveying the symbolism attached to white rice in Korea that specifically derives from the colonisation period.

Solomon doesn't understand what's happening initially, as Sunja is overcome by emotion upon realising that she's tasting Korean-grown rice. He can't taste the difference between Korean and Japanese rice, since he has eaten white rice every day of his life and has never had it withheld from him. Likewise, the symbolism of the white rice and the simplicity of its purchase and preparation like clockwork at mealtimes each day is lost on him. The multisensory experience and historical narrative aren't as relatable for him, as his experiences with colonisation have not included this aspect.

White rice was withheld from the Korean people during events of national suffering that form definitive components of Korean identity. Korea's colonisation by the Japanese was one of those that has become synonymous with Korea's rice symbolism. When Japan annexed Korea, they reserved the limited sale of the white rice produced in the country to Japanese consumers, to recover from their own rice shortage. However, in doing so they were unable to feed the colony, and so Koreans were limited to eating alternative grains, such as barley, millet, sorghum, and corn. Korean children born during colonisation grew up never tasting the white rice of their homeland.

At the same time, Korean farmers were forced to produce rice genetically engineered by the Japanese through hybridisation, which led to the extinction of the wide variety of Korean rice that had existed before. Korea has always been a predominantly agricultural country. In 1914, Keir reported that 1,400 types of indigenously Korean rice had been catalogued by the Japanese, with 75% percent of Koreans involved in farming, and 94% of the land solely devoted to rice cultivation.[8] By the end of Japanese occupation, however, hardly any remained, with Japanese varieties making up 90% of the varieties grown in Korea.[9]

## White hanbok

Our next object is white *hanbok*. Koreans are self-proclaimed *baekuiminjok* (백의민족), which means 'people of white clothes'. By the Westerners that travelled to Korea during the Joseon period, Kreans also became known as a "white-robed race",[10] with travellers remarking that regardless of gender or status, they were all dressed in white. Sometimes they wore jackets in muted blue or rose; however, all wore white inside.

While wearing all white clothing might be considered bland or simple by outsiders, for Koreans it is the complete opposite. This traditional, formal everyday wear of average Korean people is a matter of national pride; a representation of purity and integrity – or more importantly – maintaining purity and integrity when challenged. As such, when told to wear coloured garments by the Japanese, during colonisation, white became an important symbol of resistance.

*Jieun:* White *hanbok* looks unimpressive but is impressive. It all comes down to the power of visual silence – the refusal to add another colour – the resistance of outside influences, to the West, and at the time of *Pachinko* to Japanese colonial rule.

It was a particularly poignant symbol, if we consider the resilience already signified in the wearing of white traditionally by Koreans. The concept is simple: white clothing is difficult to keep clean. To wear it is representative of the endurance of a challenge, and as such an uncompromising nature – the uncompromising nature and strength of Koreans. Wearing white subsequently shows the accomplishment of this challenge, and one's good character, respectability, and integrity.

*Loli:* In many ways this appears an extension of Korean society's ideology to its visual aesthetic – a visual demonstration of the effort and diligence that is valued as a social asset, and which we also see in the rigidity of interpersonal relations as they are expressed in Korean language and culture.

Indeed, there were different contexts of resistance in the wearing of white by Koreans periodically. In the context of Japanese annexation, Koreans were instructed to wear Japanese clothes, or at least coloured clothes. In *Pachinko* (2022), there is a scene in which Sunja returns from the market and is told that there is a rumour being circulated that Korean women daring to wear white have been pelted with mud and faeces by Japanese children. She is warned to be careful, and to avoid going to the town alone.

It is important to note that in *Pachinko*, the shades of beige and cream that we see are the 'white of the day', as it is possible for viewers to find themselves confused over which *hanbok* is considered white, and subsequently how clothing choices may be meaningful or not. In an interview with *Vogue*, *Pachinko's* costume designer recently addressed this, explaining that the dyes used to create the costumes were textured organic dyes like those that Koreans used in the 1910s as opposed to modern synthetic dyes that produce the starchy whites that we are used to today.[11]

South Korean two-time Olympic medallist figure skater, Yuna Kim, recently headlined London fashion week, participating in the modelling and design of a *hanbok* collection in conjunction with ten *hanbok* design houses. The show was titled '*Hanbok Fashion Show, The Hanbok Wave*', and the *hanbok* worn by Yuna will be featured in French fashion magazine *Marie Claire* and a video from the photoshoot will be displayed on a Broadway billboard in Times Square in New York City. All importantly, the collection showcases Koreans' love of white, and 'whitened colours', such as light pastels. We see *K-* again here in the transnationalism of the '*Hanbok* Wave' – the popularity of *hanboks*, and its origins in popular culture, and participatory fandom – while a political discourse that is specific to Koreans.

*Loli:* It is interesting because on the one hand the white *hanbok* seems to be what Koreans were known for during the Joseon period, and subsequently after. On the other hand, there is also this association with *hanbok* being quite colourful, as more recently there have indeed been a wide variety of colours worn and a culture of people wearing the *hanbok* once reserved for royalty.

We see this association made in the interpretation of *hanbok* by non-Koreans who design and sell *hanbok*. For instance, fashion designer Carolina Herrera, partnered with Korea's Ministry of Culture, Sports and Tourism and the Hanbok Advancement Centre, designed three *hanbok* that merge the traditional with the contemporary, reflecting the signature aesthetic of the House of Herrera, while retaining the essence of the traditional *hanbok*.

Meanwhile, non-Korean sellers on stores like Amazon, eBay, Etsy, and AliExpress sell traditional *hanbok* too, which they market as a "colourful", "princess", "cosplay", "folk", "stage", "palace party", and "dance costume". In one example, the *hanbok* is even described using keywords such as "Japanese", "Female", "Korean", "palace", and "wedding".

## Suit, kimono, or *hanbok*?

We return to the choice of kimono, suit, or *hanbok* here. *Pachinko* is set in a similar period to *Mr Sunshine* (2018) when the politics of fashion were dynamic and could be fatal. Through the characters of *Pachinko*, we can explore the politics of fashion even further, adding the dimension of Zainichi to the equation.

Just as white *hanbok* is a symbol of resistance, so is *hanbok* itself. When Sunja emigrates to Japan, she continues to don *hanbok*, while her husband, brother-in-law, and sister-in-law all wear Western clothing. If we consider Japanese-Korean relations, Western clothing, which was popular among the Japanese already, was a more neutral option for negotiating one's visual identity at the time. It was neither a betrayal to Koreans nor a confrontation to the Japanese. However, Sunja remains constant, and Korean in this respect.

Hansu, however, who has openly sold out to the Japanese to prioritise his own survival, is shown alternating between Japanese kimono and Western suits. He is shown wearing kimono only in Japan, in flashbacks to his past (prior to his success), and in the present at home with his Japanese wife, whereas he is shown wearing Western suits in both Japan and Korea. The kimono, like speaking Japanese and behaving with Japanese etiquette, allows Hansu to blend in, and not to be distinguished from the Japanese, and subsequently discriminated against. Even two generations later, Sunja's grandson blends in so well that his bosses think he is Japanese.

Western suits provide neutrality, as well as the implication of high status. As such suits are well-suited to his role as a fish broker when he returns to Korea. He is well known and feared, and won't put up with nonsense, but he does not position himself as entirely in opposition to the Koreans either. He doesn't mercilessly belittle, nor does he intimidate, nor is he sadistic, as we often see in the depictions of Japanese treatment of the Koreans. Perhaps this is purely a way of hedging his bets

**FIGURE 6.3**  Hansu wearing a new Western suit at the fish market in Korea, in *Pachinko*. The man speaking to him (right) is visibly submissive, despite appearing older than Hansu, also indicative of feelings of fear towards him.

and ensuring his survival in both social contexts, without giving up his status, or perhaps he has empathy for his fellow Koreans which may or may not be an inner conflict. Either way, his clothing choices are not arbitrary but rather strategies for cross-culturally navigating socio-political environments.

The Western suit in the 1920s was a symbol of wealth. Although Sunja's in-laws wear Western clothes, their clothing is old and worn as their families had been wealthy before and kept some articles of clothing; this is even emphasised when Sunja's groom explains that his suit was passed on to him by his brother who died in the war, and that is why the suit is too large for him and worn out. For Sunja's in-laws' family, Western clothes provide some neutrality. Nevertheless, it indicated their wealthy status and thus implied a relationship with the Japanese too.

*Jieun:* Like the reluctance of Koreans to make kimchi in Japan, Hansu is hiding his Korean-ness. He wants to be assumed to be Japanese. This contrasts with Sunja. She has courage that he doesn't have. She doesn't lower her head as others do when Japanese policemen pass on patrol. When in dire need of money, she makes kimchi and sells it in the marketplace, even though this would be inviting discrimination, like a beacon telling everyone "I am Korean."

Sunja did not have the same experience of being a Zainichi as early into colonisation as Hansu, who witnessed Koreans being burnt alive in the massacre in Kanto at the time of the 1923 Tokyo earthquake.[12] In the novel, it doesn't say clearly, but it is apparent that Hansu learnt a lesson through his experience and dispersed with his Korean identity for survival.

We see how purposefully he has done this, even before the second season, in how Hansu switches between Western and Japanese clothing and between the Korean, Japanese, and English languages. Most importantly, when Hansu is with

FIGURE 6.4   Sunja makes and sells kimchi despite the risk to her, in *Pachinko*.

Sunja, he embodies and exposes his Korean identity for the first time. The moments they spend together are the only ones in which we see him embrace his Korean identity openly and positively.

*Loli:*  In the first season of *Pachinko*, it doesn't yet show how Hansu is involved in the *yakuza*; there are hints, such as the yakuza confronting his father who handles his accounts. This scene is disturbed by the earthquake, which kills Hansu's father, leaving him with no family. During the earthquake Hansu and the *yakuza* come together, and the *yakuza* saves Hansu's life. At the end of the episode, the *yakuza* brings Hansu to stay the night with his family, hinting at an ongoing relationship and potentially a special bond growing between the men because of their shared experience. The first season does not give any further information on the development of this relationship, however.

*Jieun:*  Yes, the book is more informative of Hansu's involvement with the *yakuza*, though we don't know how season 2 of the series will unfold yet. Without giving too many spoilers, what I can say is that being in the *yakuza*, despite its glamorisation in film and television, is not considered respectable. It does not mean that Hansu is entirely bad. He still has some good in him, and we see this in his devotion to taking care of Sunja and his son, even if secretly from the shadows.

Also, to touch briefly on another Western object, which is closely related to clothing, Hansu gives Sunja a Western pocket watch at one point as a gift. Like Western clothes, the pocket watch is something that a Korean could never own, unless they had a connection to the Japanese. This would have a negative connotation to Koreans, who would assume that having such an item would mean you have done something wrong to get it. Therefore, although season 1 is less explicit about Hansu's *yakuza* ties, this, along with his clothing and position, indicates he is involved in something bad.

*Jieun:*  The novel specifies that the pocket watch is from London, England. It is very rare and precious. The fact that Hansu gives it to Sunja is significant in expressing that he does indeed love her, even if he finds himself trapped in a situation that prevents him from marrying her.

## Television

Many Koreans who emigrated during the annexation period never returned to Korea, and either through practicality or for their own protection, they did not teach their children to speak Korean. Therefore, for many, the development of television was a way – the only way – to engage with Korean culture in a safe space.

## VHS was all we had!

VHS was especially important. While nowadays YouTube and streaming services provide an easy means of accessing Korean content, television was the only way to engage with Korean culture before the internet. If you were outside of Korea, then this meant you were reliant upon VHS.

*Jieun:* Until only about 10 years ago, in London, people would rent VHS (and eventually DVDs too) from Korean supermarkets. It was like an alternative *Blockbusters* for Korean television shows and films. Wherever there is a Korean diaspora, there is a culture of borrowing VHS at Korean supermarkets. There is a need for it to maintain their cultural identity. Obviously, since streaming came about there wasn't really a need for it anymore.

*Loli:* It must have been a means of building solidarity too.

*Jieun:* Yes, you borrow and watch together. Likewise, rice cookers, you cook rice in your rice cookers and eat together.

*Loli:* In this way, objects are a really important place to begin conversations about *K-*. Their importance is shown in how Koreans gather around them to feel solidarity among countrymen, while fans participate in them to feel solidarity among fandoms.

*Jieun:* Many of these objects, and buildings too, are like cornerstones in the communities of the Korean diaspora. In New York, for instance, there is a Korean town. There, Korean people eat Korean food, borrow Korean VHS or DVDs, shop at Korean supermarkets and chemists; they even have a public bath. I experienced this when I visited New York in 2006. This was in central New York, not far from the Empire State Building. I was especially shocked to find that they had a public bath, as in London an attempt to open one was unsuccessful.

*Loli:* Is Korea town like Korea itself?

*Jieun:* There are Korean things there that make Koreans feel more at home, but it is more like stepping into a nostalgic Korea – they kept what they remembered of the Korea they knew. So, it is often more like 1990s Korea, or earlier. This is just what I observed.

## Then streaming opened everything up!

The shift from VHS to streaming services was incredibly important to the extension of *K-*. Prior to streaming, Korean content was just for Koreans. This is not to say that non-Koreans were unwelcome, but simply non-Koreans wouldn't know where a Korean supermarket was, let alone think of renting out Korean films on VHS. The fandom was so marginal that there wasn't enough interest to attract a wider audience. Now, however, with the easy access of streaming, and subsequent mainstream status, the objects people are engaging with, searching for, and adopting in their daily lives are changing dramatically.

*Jieun:*  During the VHS era, K-dramas and K-films were just a way for Koreans to stay connected. Online sharing and streaming, especially Netflix, have transformed the way we engage with Korean content. All the things that were once relevant to only Koreans are now relevant to everyone everywhere who consumes the K-Wave.

The shift from VHS to streaming services is transforming much more than our experience with popular culture. It is making way for the adoption of Korean cultural preferences and customs, which are aspects of the traditional side of Korean content that Koreans might not have imagined would be so eagerly adopted. As we have seen, traditional clothing, like the *hanbok*, has been well received. On websites such as Amazon.co.uk, Etsy.com, and eBay, you can purchase traditional Korean items that entirely lack a cultural context for their use beyond Korean households. *Hanbok* is perhaps the most notable, with even babies and children's *hanbok* for sale. Since babies and young children are not likely to be actively joining K-pop fandom anytime soon, we can only assume that either Korean diaspora are becoming an important demographic to cater to, or that non-Koreans are buying *hanbok* for their babies and children.

Perhaps more surprisingly, there is also a considerable range of *Doljabi* ritual sets, *100 Days Party* sets, and *Doljanchi* sets for sale at online stores like Etsy.com and Amazon. The *Doljanchi* party (also known as *'Dol'*) is a ceremony held on a child's first birthday, which is said to bless the child with a prosperous future. At the ceremony, a ritual called *Doljabi* is performed, which involves the child choosing from a tray of items that is said to foretell the child's future. A traditional *Doljabi* set consists of a bow, coins in a pouch, a medallion, a brush, yarn, five colour paper, a medicine pot, a rice ball, and a notebook. Today sets vary, with some including cameras, microphones, and calligraphy pens. There is also the *100 Days Party*, which is held when a baby reaches its 100th day following birth. This is an ancient

**FIGURE 6.5**  Traditional *Doljabi* set featured in *Pachinko*.

FIGURE 6.6    A typical *Dol* celebration. All items on the table can now be purchased easily online around the globe.

custom which arose when the infant mortality rate was much higher. Both the *100 Days Party* and *Doljanchi* involve the preparation of a table, upon which is food for guests (e.g., cake, fruits, and other Korean snacks), decorations (e.g., balls of yarn and flowers), and a seat that the baby sits in for a photograph. Sets like these are available on Etsy, many of which include imitation cakes and snacks for the purpose of photography, rather than actual food. Whether this subtlety is the evolution of the tradition for non-Koreans, a feasible version for diaspora, or *K-* needs further investigation. It is early days for many of these emerging factions of the K-Wave.

This phenomenon is not limited to online shopping either. Traditional Korean baby clothes, which are wrapped and tied instead of buttoned or done up with poppers, are being sold at popular high-street clothing store, H&M. Moreover, they are described as 'Korean baby clothes', and are searchable as such on Google.

*Jieun:*    Korean dramas especially are responsible for transmitting aspects of Korean life. The boundary has been destabilised, so that *100 Days Parties* are being held by people without any background in Korea. It's all related: you read, you watch, you buy. It's that simple.

*Loli:*    This is also a very positive development for the diaspora, and an interesting circulation of Korean culture. The internet allowed the masses to engage with Korean content, popularising words and objects, and as a result Korean culture could be brought back to the diaspora, as well as stimulating their environments to become more Korea-friendly. How do you think this level of infiltration into Western culture has been achieved?

*Jieun:*    K-pop idols really built a strong foundation for the K-Wave to go global. Of course, over time the content developed and extended to various forms of media. Netflix built upon this foundation, with people of all ages and sentiments following the K-Wave. This is something that wasn't possible with other waves. The Japanese Wave, for instance, was not so straightforward. J-pop didn't have the consumer range that K-pop has had, and so they couldn't gain enough momentum to snowball into the mainstream.

*Loli:* I suppose a good question is, what precisely non-Korean consumers are getting that motivates them to engage with Korean cultural products at this level?

*Jieun:* When it comes to things like *Doljabi*, I believe there is influence from the Korean diaspora there. I think that there must be some Korean heritage for supply and demand to arise in the first place. This may take the form of non-Korean in-laws being inspired by their experiences with their Korean family member's culture. People might feel proud to take part. It is like my family's tradition of making dumplings at Christmas time. My British in-laws have me, so we make that our tradition.

*Loli:* My sister-in-law is Taiwanese. She joined our family when I was a child, and so I was fortunate to participate in Lunar New Year festivities each year. She gave me a *cheongsam* to wear at one of my brother's weddings. My mother, father, great-aunts and uncles, their neighbours, and friends from the local community have all taken part in certain aspects of Chinese culture through her. There is a lot of enjoyment in it, in the inclusivity, and a certain pride that comes with that. There is a lot to be said for feeling welcomed by another culture and to let go of your inhibitions and enjoy that experience.

Lunar New Year is a good example of how traditions can be transferred and become a part of the lives of people in other cultures. I have noticed British people eagerly taking part in Lunar New Year since I was a teenager, whether they have a family member who inspired their interest or not. I remember attending a Lunar New Year event in 2008 at a club in London that famously held a big event each year. There were many East Asian partygoers, but there were also many British ones too.

## Landscape

There is much to be said about the landscape in *Pachinko*, and indeed in all Korean dramas and films. Since little has been explored about landscape and identity in Korean content, we make this our next object. First, it is important that we define precisely what we mean by landscape. We refer to the environment in which events are set; both interior and exterior.

Landscape is intrinsically interwoven into identity and nation.[13] When you are far from home, the landscape remains in our memories, and when we return, we can feel that we are home with all our senses. Familiar sights, smells, sounds, and even textures, become parts of our identity that give us a feeling of belonging.

### The sea

For diaspora the sea is a landscape that signifies a complex part of their identity. The sea represents both home and away and can recall associations of the known and unknown, loss and gain, conflicting emotions, and conflicting cultures, which diasporas spend their lifetime negotiating. Sunja is from Busan, which is located at the southeastern tip of the Korean Peninsula. Therefore, for Sunja, the landscape of the seaside holds poignancy. It isn't only a signifier of home and away in that it represents leaving Korean soil for another land, but rather that the seaside itself is her home.

The objects that construct her Korean identity can be collected from the visual and sound footage from there and from her home. The sea itself is first. She catches abalone, just as the *haenyeo* (해녀) 'female divers' of Jeju Island who often come to mind when one thinks of free diving. These memories of being in the sea as a child often involve her father. When he passes away, she walks fully clothed into the sea, demonstrating a connection between herself, him, and the sea. The two spent a great deal of time there together, and the sea feels like home, so this landscape holds great importance to Sunja's identity.

### The fish market

The fish market is perhaps as significant as the sea to Sunja. In the series, the marketplace is the setting of many scenes. As a young child, Sunja is shown with her father at the fish market, and in transit between there and home. As a teenager, she is known well at the fish market, and feels confident in spending time there, despite the presence of Japanese police. On each occasion, the camera follows Sunja through the marketplace. She hears familiar sounds of buying and selling and sees faces she knows well.

When Sunja finally returns to the fish market as an elderly woman, she is both surprised at the way things have changed and at home in the familiarity of the sights and smells. This is somewhat universally relatable, but there is also some unique significance for Koreans who left Korea for Japan. Many Koreans never returned to Korea after Japan surrendered, and so this scene is a familiar one for Koreans: the elderly returning to Korea for the first time.

### Eomma's house

Sunja's mother's house is the final stop on our journey of objects in this chapter. When Sunja leaves her mother's home for the last time, about to embark on a voyage with her new husband to Osaka, she turns and looks back at her mother's home. A series of brief shots of the rooms and items in the house then follow: one pile of nearly folded mattresses, and then another, and then a shot of the room; her mother's bed, her bed, in the place she was raised.

The multisensory characteristics of these objects are relevant to Koreans. The image of the bedding remains in Sunja's memory of her home. Each day, she would have folded the bedding in the morning and laid them out at night, as goes the

Korean custom. This practice is no different than the image Sunja keeps in her memory, in fact it may be more important since she can re-create the practice wherever she goes. The practices that involve the objects are subsequently powerful emotional conduits and provide further layers of Korean-ness and *K-* to explore.

*Loli:* Interestingly, Korean (often labelled as 'Japanese') mattresses seem to be increasingly accessible for non-Koreans. Amazon, for instance, sells a multitude, which was not the case even 5 years ago. This was not inspired by the *Pachinko* series, since it was released so recently, but there is clearly more of a climate for these products or else they wouldn't be available.

## Notes

1  James, Caryn. 2022. "Pachinko Review: A 'Dazzling, Heartfelt Korean Epic'." *BBC Culture*. www.bbc.com/culture/article/20220323-pachinko-review-a-dazzling-heartfelt-korean-epic

2  Emmys. 2022. "Pachinko Awards & Nominations." *Emmys.Com*. www.emmys.com/shows/pachinko

3  Goyal, Darshita. 2022. "In Apple TV+ Drama *Pachinko*, the Costumes Symbolise a Changing Korean Identity." *Vogue*. www.vogue.in/fashion/content/in-apple-tv-drama-pachinko-the-costumes-symbolise-a-changing-korean-identity

4  Kim, Soon Hee, Myung Sunny Kim, Myoung Sook Lee, Yong Soon Park, Hae Jeong Lee, Soon-ah Kang, Hyun Sook Lee, et al. 2016. "Korean Diet: Characteristics and Historical Background." *Journal of Ethnic Foods*, 3(1), pp. 26–31. https://doi.org/10.1016/j.jef.2016.03.002

5  Kim, Soon Hee, Myung Sunny Kim, Myoung Sook Lee, Yong Soon Park, Hae Jeong Lee, Soon-ah Kang, Hyun Sook Lee, et al. 2016. "Korean Diet: Characteristics and Historical Background." *Journal of Ethnic Foods*, 3(1), pp. 26–31. https://doi.org/10.1016/j.jef.2016.03.002

6  Kim, Soon Hee, Myung Sunny Kim, Myoung Sook Lee, Yong Soon Park, Hae Jeong Lee, Soon-ah Kang, Hyun Sook Lee, et al. 2016. "Korean Diet: Characteristics and Historical Background." *Journal of Ethnic Foods*, 3(1), pp. 26–31. https://doi.org/10.1016/j.jef.2016.03.002

7  Kim, Soon Hee, Myung Sunny Kim, Myoung Sook Lee, Yong Soon Park, Hae Jeong Lee, Soon-ah Kang, Hyun Sook Lee, et al. 2016. "Korean Diet: Characteristics and Historical Background." *Journal of Ethnic Foods*, 3(1), pp. 26–31. https://doi.org/10.1016/j.jef.2016.03.002

8  Kwon, Mee-yoo. 2020. "'Parasite' Subtitle Translator Becomes Busan Honorary Citizen." *The Korea Times*. www.koreatimes.co.kr/www/art/2020/04/689_288258.html

9  Kwon, Mee-yoo. 2020. "'Parasite' Subtitle Translator Becomes Busan Honorary Citizen." *The Korea Times*. www.koreatimes.co.kr/www/art/2020/04/689_288258.html

10 Baihui, Duan. 2019. "Subtle Changes in the Joseon's Everyday Life Based on the Westerners' Discourses (1800–1880)." *The Review of Korean Studies*, 22(1).

11 Goyal, Darshita. 2022. "In Apple TV+ Drama *Pachinko*, the Costumes Symbolise a Changing Korean Identity." *Vogue*. www.vogue.in/fashion/content/in-apple-tv-drama-pachinko-the-costumes-symbolise-a-changing-korean-identity

12 Ryang, Sonia. 2005. "The Tongue That Divided Life and Death. The 1923 Tokyo Earthquake and the Massacre of Koreans." *The Asia-Pacific Journal*, 5(9). https://apjjf.org/-Sonia-Ryang/2513/article.html

13 Darby, Wendy Joy. 2000. *Landscape and Identity: Geographies of Nation and Class in England: V. 9* (Materializing Culture). London: Bloomsbury.

# 7

# KIM JI-YOUNG: BORN 1982

Kim Do-young's *82 Nyeonsaeng Gim Jiyeong* (82년생 김지영) 'Kim Ji-young: Born 1982' (2019) is the movie adaptation of the bestselling novel by Cho Nam-Joo. The novel chronicles the life of a woman desperate to escape the restrictive traditional conceptualisations of gender roles in South Korea, which triggered combat over sexism in South Korea.

*Kim Ji-young: Born 1982* tells the story of Ji-young (also romanised *Ji-yeong*), a typical Korean mother, who has given up her career to be a stay-at-home mum and finds the expectation for her to do so and the gender inequality in her everyday life to be stifling. She develops a delusional disorder, where for short periods she believes she is her own mother, or at times her grandmother. She has no memory of the episodes and for a long time only her husband 'knows about it'.

The film also tells the story of Korean family dynamics. Even if Ji-young is unhappy being a stay-at-home-mum, she cannot change it easily. Even though Ji-young's husband offers to be a househusband, there is pressure from his family for him to fulfil his role as the provider, and he has to navigate between the hierarchy and desires of his wife and his parents. The need to do so isn't as strong in the West because concepts like filial piety do not exist there, nor does the rest of the Confucian interpersonal relations system that characterises Korean relations and therefore all aspects of their daily lives.

## Contemporary Korean womanhood and K-

*Loli:* Why do you feel Ji-young's story resonated with so many globally?

*Jieun:* Gender imbalance, like social inequality in *Squid Game*, is a global issue. It is presented in a Korean context; that's where the hybridity of *K-* arises, in how the issue is peppered with the unique quirks of Korean culture.

DOI: 10.4324/9781003203230-7

*Loli:*   It has the benefit of providing both resonance and intrigue. A simple choice of location or action, like the wearing of an apron or the peeling of fruit, holds so much meaning and can stimulate so much curiosity. It creates a complex discourse that requires some knowledge of the tension between ancient and contemporary Korean society, as it is demonstrative of the dissonance that has developed because of both modernisation and Westernisation. It almost seems that a blank space is created by the cross-cultural gap, stimulating intrigue in a familiar subject. In this respect, the experience of *K-* by non-Koreans in film viewing is a lot like enjoying a remake, only instead of the narrative being reinterpreted, we are also seeing reinterpretations of societal issues which are of course much more impactful than the stories of individuals.

*Jieun:*   Also, in this case, the societal issues are quite multidimensional and particular in their construction because of neo-Confucianism. By this I mean that in Korea, men have also had a difficult time. Neo-Confucian voices in societal discourse tell men that they must take the role of provider or otherwise bring shame upon their family, must not do housework because that is for women, and mustn't show emotion or seek affection. As well as causing tensions in marriages, this also means that men cannot do otherwise whether they want to or not. In the West, these views are considered outdated, and so the way men relate may be different, but the multidimensionality of hierarchy and how it affects people in Korea – the weight of responsibility and obedience on either respective party – opens the possibility for the narrative to resonate with male viewers too.

*Loli:*   Husbands' families are also often expected to buy newlywed couples their first home, while wives' families are expected to buy the furniture. Men must submit to military conscription, while women do not. Men consider the loss of time as unfair, as it delays or interrupts their university studies or delays their entrance to the workforce. Many arguments are often presented by Korean men to this effect, that feminists in Korea essentially want to have their cake and eat it too; with their desire to not be conscripted, and to receive a home as a gift from their in-laws, while not being subjected to gender-based traditions like cooking the foods during national holidays and taking maternity leave but still being considered for promotions like their male counterparts who do not need to do so.

*Jieun:*   Even though Confucianist ideologies specify hierarchies, the Korean language was already equipped with considerable tools for fulfilling the needs of a highly hierarchical society. It is very much a 'chicken and egg' situation, and we don't know which one came first. However, whether it is language or society that makes Korean society so hierarchical, it exists; and because of that men and women have a difficult time. Ji-young's husband suffers for this very reason. He is in a really difficult situation, because his family and friends have expectations that he should go to work and Ji-young should stay at home to care for their child. He wants to take leave and give Ji-young the chance to go back to work, to benefit her mental health; however, his family is not supportive or sensitive towards this. Maintaining gender roles is more important to them than the individual needs of men and women.

## #MeToo

Many think that it was this book that triggered the South Korean #MeToo movement, but the book was published in 2016, after the #MeToo movement had already begun in South Korea. *Kim Ji-young: Born 1982* is underpinned by the politics of the women's liberation front, instead of the #MeToo movement – addressing issues concerning the sexist practices that women in South Korea encounter in their everyday routines, from housework to feminine beauty practices. This is a different societal issue to the misogyny and sexual abuse, which is the target of the #MeToo movement.

*Jieun:* In contemporary South Korean society, schoolchildren learn that they are equal, but, at the same time, are shown that they are not. In the Korean school curriculum, from the age of 13 years, Practical Studies is taught with girls and boys separated into groups. The girls are taught to cook and sew, and the boys are taught to fix things. Then, as they grow up, they experience for themselves that there is no equality between the sexes and between in-laws. In one scene, there is a conversation between both of Ji-young's grandmothers. Ji-young's father's mother is clearly the boss, while Ji-young's mother's mother is quite powerless. Other hierarchies in Korean society, all which are underpinned by Confucian philosophy on how to conduct interpersonal relations in society, present similar issues, such as ageism in age hierarchy.

This is moreover a situation not unique to Korea but found generally in societies that practice Confucianism. Many of the most systematic and institutionalised sexist ideologies have been claimed to originate from the Confucian philosophy of 'filial piety'. On womanhood and Confucianism in China, Li argues:

"The most systematic, institutionalised, and deep-rooted sexist ideologies and practices in China originated from the philosophy of "filial piety" of Confucius (551–479 B.C.). The three components of "filial piety" stipulated that women must obey men; citizens must obey their ruler and the young must obey the elderly. For thousands of years, the rules of these three obediences helped maintain the patriarchal social order in China. Abusive practices and behaviors such as the sale and purchase of women, wife-beating, and female infanticide were not uncommon."[1]

FIGURE 7.1   Ji-young experiences discrimination even from her own father, who gives favourable treatment to his son, as is Confucian philosophy, in *Kim Ji-young: Born 1982*.

These same sentiments towards men and women are seen in *Kim Ji-young: Born 1982* (2019). The film highlights that Ji-young has experienced discrimination throughout her life, in every facet of her socialisation – by her parents, in the workplace, professionally in respect to her career choices, and even by strangers. Discrimination is present at the dinner table, in the gifts she receives or doesn't receive from her father in comparison to her brother, in how she is supported and celebrated in sad and happy times.

### Female voices

Our first object is the female voice, both spoken and heard by women.

*Loli:*   *Kim Ji-young: Born 1982* aims to provide us with a picture of everyday Korean womanhood. As a Korean woman, what concepts or memories does the story bring up for you?

*Jieun:*   When I watch the scene where Kim Ji-young, her mother, sister, and grandmothers (including her mother's mother-in-law), I really feel that women make other women's lives difficult. They are the main antagonists. There is lots of interesting communication between these women, in which they maintain the traditions that oppress themselves. Women's relationship with the neo-Confucian ethos is paradoxical in this respect. Ji-young's mother-in-law has sympathy for own daughter when she works hard for her in-laws, but not for her daughter-in-law, even though she herself has been a daughter-in-law and so knows the pain all too well.

I have personal experience of this. On many occasions, my mother makes all the decisions, and then when I try to help my mother tells me I only come once per year so take rest. Then, everyone goes to the living room, while my sister-in-law does all the work.

*Loli:*  We see this reflected when Ji-young's husband is very understanding and tries to avoid situations where these old customs take place, but in the social context he can't help. His wife is forced to bear the pressure of society to

FIGURE 7.2   Three generations of women, including Ji-young, her mother, her maternal grandmother, and her paternal grandmother, in *Kim Ji-young: Born 1982*.

FIGURE 7.3   Ji-young works diligently in the kitchen throughout *Chuseok*, while everyone rests and spends time together, in *Kim Ji-young: Born 1982*.

save her family's face. Likewise, her mother-in-law is also under pressure from society to exercise her power over her daughter-in-law. Being able to do so, for both women, is a practice of creating the ideal both within their family activities and to the outside world.

*Jieun:* This makes women very vulnerable, and during national holidays Korean women are known for suffering from depression, severe stress, and burn-out; often summarised under a single term in Korea – 'holiday syndrome'. I was telling my mother and sister about the narrative of this film, and my mother assured me that there are much worse cases. She told me in the old days she had to do much more. What is interesting is that men are not involved in this, but it is rather a women's power game.

## Women should work without rest, except when eating

*Jieun:* When I see Ji-young not being able to enjoy the holidays, it always makes me think of the *So Hae Wang Eun* (소해왕은), which means 'women should work without rest, except when eating'.

This saying is from *Naehun* (내훈) 'Admonishments for Women'.[2] Considered a representative book among those that present Confucian ideals on the social construction of gender and sexuality in premodern East Asia, *Naehun* is a manual that instructs women on their gender and how to behave accordingly. It was written by Queen Insu and published in 1475. As you can imagine the ideology clashes greatly with 21st-century Korea, despite underpinning much of the customs and preferences that relate to gender in Korea today.

*Jieun:* Confucian philosophies like these are unfair, and I often wonder why we make life hard for ourselves. I think, ultimately, in contemporary Korea, it has become more of a habit than anything else. Though, interestingly, once taking on a task, mothers typically then ask their daughters or (if they have any) daughters-in-law to do the work. I have experienced this first-hand. My mother wants to go to great lengths to prepare for the holiday, but it is me and my sister-in-law who do the labour – especially my sister-in-law. She never complains, and seems not to mind at all, and yet she spends the whole time in the kitchen cooking, then serving, then washing-up.

*Kim Ji-young: Born 1982* particularly shows the difficulties of contemporary womanhood regarding labour. In the past, being a 'good' wife and mother – according to the Korean ideal – was feasible. Women were at home full-time, and there wasn't the same hunger for a career and success that there is among women today. There weren't professional female role models, nor the pressure for them to succeed professionally. However, in contemporary Korea, working mothers bear the weight of professional pressures and desires, while traditional domestic expectations remain. The situation simply isn't feasible, leading to situations like the one Ji-young finds herself in: having to end a promising career to devote herself to motherhood, all the while watching the women without children around her excel professionally.

*Loli:*   There has not been an equal shift in the expectations of men to evolve in their roles, now that wives are contributing to the family's income. Women's work has increased, and these new types of work take place in highly competitive working and educational environments. Women are expected to compete in education, and then for promotions, and for salaries. Men taking part in household chores can be perceived as unattractive, and wives are often blamed for this. We see this in the film.

*Jieun:*   Indeed, womanhood in the everyday lives of married women, and especially those who have children, seems to turn women into real-life Korean Cinderellas. However, without the sympathy of home audiences, because this situation is the status quo in Korea, it is very unlikely that a daughter-in-law or her husband would confront his parents. The continuation of gendered customs sometimes feels almost vengeful, "I did it, now you do it!" In fact, this is so serious that one often hears stories of divorces caused by issues with in-laws. This is very different from the West.

Korean in-laws have a senior position and are traditionally able to instruct their children and children-in-law on how to behave. Between in-laws and daughters-in-law, the situation is most severe, because serving your husband's parents is traditionally more important than serving your own parents. We see this in *Kim Ji-young: Born 1982*, when Ji-young is unable to leave her in-laws easily to go to her family's home to spend time with them at Chuseok (Korean mid-autumn festival) too. Her in-laws show little thought towards Ji-young's feelings or needs.

*Loli:*   I have often observed the need to make the daughter-in-law busy. If she is seen to be resting or socialising comfortably for too long, she will be urged to do another task or offer help to another person. This is not something that really goes on normally in Western households. Cleaning and cooking simply aren't involved in the in-law relationship, except for when one offers to do something to help or be nice on a family occasion. There are certainly no repercussions upon a woman who does not wash up after every meal, or who asks someone else to do so when she doesn't want to. If anything, there is a pressure on everyone else to take their turn, regardless of age or gender. The concept of fairness extends to everyone, and superiority is replaced by courtesy and kindness to those who might be more tired than you, perhaps because they are elderly or have cooked dinner, so you offer to wash up.

*Jieun:*   Korean in-laws are well known for turning up unannounced, letting themselves into your home (because in Korea we unlock our front doors with passwords instead of keys), and then ordering you around. It is an invasion of space that you do not normally find in Western relationships. Moreover, when they do this, the son- or daughter-in-law is not able to refuse or complain, because it isn't socially acceptable for them to do so.

It isn't just the daughter-in-law who must be obedient; mothers-in-law also tend to be quite particular about how they want things done. Again, this reflects original neo-Confucianism from Joseon times, when the kitchen was the woman's space. Mothers and mothers-in-law like to assume control over *their* kitchen and their daughter-in-law in the kitchen. The basic unspoken rule is that one's mother-in-law is always right, and there is no negotiation over this. There is no "when in Rome" attitude, no matter where the cooking takes place. Instead, just do what your mother-in-law wants you to do. Proposing otherwise would be unthinkable and would cause serious problems. In the past, doing so would even be considered a form of not taking care of your parents-in-law well, and could be grounds for a husband to divorce his wife.

*Loli:* The foods themselves are labour-intensive and numerous – prepared by the women, offered to the men, received by the ancestors, and eaten by the family.

Among the most popular dishes are traditional rice cakes, such as *songpyeon* (송편); a half-moon-shaped rice cake; and beet *songpyeon*, a sweet rice cake coloured with beetroot. *Japchae* (잡채) is a dish often present during festive days in Korea, especially *Chuseok*. *Japchae* is a compound word made of words *'jap'* (잡), meaning mix, and *'chae'* (채), from *chaeso* (채소) which means vegetable. *Japchae* is made by mixing various vegetables together with meat and glass noodles.

There are numerous battered foods served at *Chuseok*, too, such as, *modeumjeon* (모듬전); battered and pan-fried slices of zucchini, shrimp, and fish, *yukjeon* (육전); battered pan-fried beef, *gogi wanjajeon* (고기 완자전); battered pan-fried meatballs; and *jeon* (전) 'Korean pancake', made by mixing a variety of ingredients with a flour batter and then frying in a pan. *Jeon* is typically either made with a single ingredient, such as *dongtae jeon* (동태전) 'pollack pancake' and *hobak jeon* (호박전) 'batter-fried summer squash', or a mixture of two to three ingredients such as *haemul pajeon* (해물파전) 'seafood and green onion pancake' and *kimchi jeon* (김치전) 'kimchi pancake'. Another variation of *jeon* is *kkaennip* jeon (깻잎전), which are stuffed with a meat mixture and wrapped in perilla leaves. Then there is *nokdujeon* (녹두전), also known as *nokdu bindaetteok* (녹두 빈대떡), which is a sweet pancake made with ground mung beans (*nokdu* in Korean).

*Jieun:* From my personal experience, my mum and aunts worked hard. My grandmother was famous in her village for food. My mum and aunts would stay up until midnight the day before *Chuseok*, making hundreds of pancakes. Eventually my mother said she couldn't eat another pancake. Meanwhile, the men didn't do anything.

Even in Britain, there are some laborious activities for women at Christ-mas; however, in my experience it takes far less time than in Korea. Korean women cook, serve, and wash up repeatedly for 3 days. Then, there is ancestral worship, which requires more special food to be prepared.

*Loli:*  One of the difficulties is that these practices are wrapped up in Korean identity. This means that there is a tension between wanting to take part – whether it be for solidarity, embracing one's culture, or to fulfil a particular cultural fantasy (the perfect picture of how things should be) – and wanting equality.

Even as a British woman married to a Korean man, I have experienced this. There is constant friction inside – an inner struggle – between wanting to take part and be a member of the group, and to embody the ideal, while at the same time wanting to feel that I am not being discriminated against because of my gender. The motivation for this is slightly different to that which stimulates the compliance of Korean women, of course. The expec-tation of those beyond immediate family is that as a Westerner will upset the accepted (preferred) social dynamic, not fit in well, and cause discom-fort for others. People always compliment me when they see that I know my place, and they compliment my husband, and his parents on this, which seems to please everyone. Ultimately, it benefits me. Another factor is that, over time, cross-cultural empathy has accumulated, and aspects of Korean culture have been influential to a degree that has developed my identity as a member of a Korean and British multicultural and bilingual family. Having children played a big part in the latter factor.

## Apron

Our next object is the apron, or *apchima* (앞치마) as it is known in Korean. Aprons have been symbolic of different things throughout history, with practical, ritual-istic, and decorative uses. Ancient Egyptians are illustrated wearing triangular aprons that hung down the front of their *schenti* by the Middle Kingdom period (*c.*2000–*c.*1500 BC).[3] The apron looked like a pyramid, with the pointy tip at the waistline and the flat base at the knee. Depictions of Koreans wearing aprons are suggested as dating back to as early as AD 357.[4] A woman wearing a white apron is depicted working in a kitchen in the Goguryeo mural painting *Anak Tomb No. 3* in Korea, located in North Korea, which is dated 357.[5]

Records of apron wearing in Europe only began during the 1300s, and despite being identified in domestic images in the *Anak Tomb No. 3*, it wasn't until the 1300s that the apron prominently became a symbol of domesticity. The Joseon era painting *Dano Poongjeong* (단오풍정) 'Scenery on Dano Day' by the famous Joseon painter Sin Yun-bok (1758–1813) depicts a group of Korean *gisaeng* (기생) entertainers bathing and washing their hair in a mountain stream. In the painting, a lady can be seen donning an apron while carrying washing wrapped in a bundle on her head.

FIGURE 7.4   An idealised image of the Korean wife and mother. Image courtesy of Cho Hyekyoung who lives in Seoul. In this image she is shown preparing side dishes on her dinner table and fruit to follow dinner.

In more recent history, aprons have signified housewifery and sexism. In the West, following World War II, the stereotypical image of a woman was her doing household chores happily while wearing an apron. Korea has developed a similar image, though whether this has been influenced by Western culture is somehow unknown; especially since early depictions of apron wearing in domestic duties, such as that in the mural painting *Anak Tomb No. 3*, suggest the practical use existed earlier than the first depictions in European.

In contemporary Korea, aprons are often a symbol of the ideal Korean housewife. The kitchen is still thought of as a woman's area, and household chores are considered primarily a woman's task, or at least idealised as so. The apron fits in well with this image.

*Jieun:* There is quite a defining scene in the film, in which Ji-young's mother-in-law gives her a gift at *Chuseok* – an apron. This isn't really a gift for her. She will wear it for the thankless hard work that she must do for her in-laws. It is just a tool for her to fulfil her role, to practically and visually fulfil the neo-Confucian fantasy of what a daughter-in-law should be.

Something as simple as who wears the apron can signify a lot. For example, a man wearing an apron would be very rare and very modern. It is like how in *The Housemaid* (1960), the husband cooks curry rice for the family. It is used to characterise him as exceptionally caring and kind beyond what is expected. The director may have deliberately added the husband cooking to make Korean viewers sympathetic towards him, even though he is having an adulterous affair with the housemaid.

A man wearing an apron can also be used to negatively characterise him as inappropriately feminine and subsequently a failure. We see an example of this in the comedy film *Miseuteo Jubu Kwizeuwang* (미스터 주부퀴즈왕) 'Mr Housewife'/'Quiz King' (2005). *Mr Housewife* tells the story of Jin-man, a househusband who, to the dismay of his career-woman wife, enjoys taking care of their daughter and doing housework. In the film, tasks like those Ji-young undertakes at *Chuseok* (e.g., food preparation, remaining in 'female spaces', like the kitchen), her behaviours, and even clothing, are utilised to characterise Ji-man as feminine or 'wife-like'.

The fact that these activities are used to symbolise femininity is evidence of the powerful association, expectations, and idealism in Korea when it comes to women, and particularly wives and mothers. Ji-man is frequently shown wearing

FIGURE 7.5   Ji-man donning his apron, and Korean washing-up gloves, and tasting kimchi while making. A common image, and one associated with Korean traditional womanhood, in *Mr Housewife/Quiz King*.

FIGURE 7.6    Ji-young dons a matching apron to her mother-in-law, and the tasting of food with hands while preparing, in *Kim Ji-young: Born 1982*.

an apron, as well as other tools associated with housewifery, such as washing-up gloves. Ji-man's daughter is even bullied at school because of her father's supposedly feminine behaviours. On the way to school one morning, her dad asks *"Apparang jibe itneungeot sileo?"* (아빠랑 집에 있는것 싫어?) 'Don't you like being with daddy at home?' Then Dana gets on the school bus, where children in her class, having observed her father bringing her to the school bus instead of her mother, sing tauntingly:

*"Jo Dana appaga eommaeyo!"*
조다나 아빠가 엄마에요
'Cho Dana has a daddy for a mummy'

We see similar concepts conveyed in the dialogue in *Kim Ji-young: Born 1982*.

*"Ye eolraga nagaseo beolmyeon eolmana beolgetseupnikka?"*
(예 얼라가 나가서 벌면 얼마나 벌겠습니까?)
'Even if this small person goes out and earns money, how much can she earn?'

*"A geu sesang nampyeoneul yukahyujikeul naego geu jipeseo nolara geuraneunge geuge mali doenya igeojiyo"*
(아 그 세상 남편을 육아휴직을 내고 그 집에서 놀아라 그라는게 그게 말이 되냐 이거지요.)
'Does it make sense to ask your husband to take paternity leave, and make him stay at home and just do nothing?'

*"Gaman ana iteora. neoneun mwo sidaekeseo noldawatna"*
(가만 앉아 있어라. 너는 뭐 시댁에서 놀다왔나.)
'Just sit down. You didn't do anything at your in-laws house.'

Some may dismiss the idea as a universal concept of motherhood or wifery, because of its practical association with the tasks that these roles entail. Indeed, the apron still holds connotations of housewifery around the world, including the West. However, in regions like the West, the concept of housewifery is not thought of as a positive anymore, and as such, the symbolism of the apron and the feelings that it evokes are far more negative when considered in the context of female identity. In Korea, aprons are symbolic of not only a woman being a mother and wife, but of a 'good wife' and a 'good mother', rather than a 'classic' or 'retro' housewife, in its embodiment of the feminine diligence idealised culturally. This ideal is made evident in the content produced by YouTube vloggers that brand themselves to attract viewers who idealise this embodiment. Many of these vloggers call themselves a 'homebody', meaning a person satisfied with the simple aspects of daily life at home, such as cooking, cleaning, and grocery shopping. Among them, the wives wear aprons as a form of branding themselves, even colour co-ordinating their aprons with their washing-up gloves.

'꿀주부 *Honeyjubu*', who as of 28 June 2022 had 1.57 million subscribers, is a representative example of many vloggers who use 'gender tools', like the apron, as branding strategies, in order to present an idealised image of womanhood to successfully market themselves.[6] We can make this link not only based on the obvious branding in the title of her videos and the subject matter but in the written narration, in which she talks about feeding and caring for her husband.

집에 있다보면 자꾸만 늘어지고 싶을 때가 있는데

FIGURE 7.7   Hamimommy co-ordinates the colour of her apron and gloves, in 'Daily Cleaning Routine to keep the house clean ǀ Housework Motivation VLOG ǀ Home Cooking Recipes' (2021).

배고픈 남편을 위해 맛있는 점심을 준비해요.
I prepare a delicious lunch for my hungry husband.

**FIGURE 7.8**  Honeyjubu's narration explains that she is preparing food for her husband, in *Honeyjubu* 꿀주부.

The importance of the apron in Honeyjubu's videos cannot be simply dismissed as practical. She, like many 'homebody' vloggers, never shows her face, nor do we hear her voice. For these women, clothing and objects are largely responsible for conveying their personalities, with only a little support from written narration. Indeed, for 꿀주부 *Honeyjubu*, the apron takes centre stage along with whatever task she is doing. She co-ordinates her apron with her surroundings, activities, or the season. In one respect, the apron appears to be a uniform for her daily tasks; however, in another respect it serves in the place of her face – it is the only thing she uses to reflect her personality, emotion, and identity. She could have chosen anything, but she chose an apron.

Other homebody vloggers, like *planD*플랜디 for example, who has 1.34 million subscribers, brand themselves as a 'homebody', and rarely, if ever, wear an apron.[7] Vlogger *planD*플랜디 conducts similar tasks to Honeyjubu and uses a similar composition – no face, no voice, written narration, similar picturesque homebody activities – however, she often wears pyjamas or cute clothes. In stark contrast to the wife/mother vloggers, she eats food from her bed. She is marketing herself to unmarried women who enjoy these simple home pleasures without serving a husband or caring for children. This, again, reinstates the association between the idealised Korean housewife and the apron.

Hamimommy, who has 1.95 million subscribers, has striking similarities to Honeyjubu in the use of the apron.[8] This vlogger is again branding herself as an idealised wife and mother, with similar subjects included in her videos, and similar composition. Though, unlike Honeyjubu, she does sometimes briefly show her face when conducting tasks that appear to require it. Hamimommy's apron is her representative as she

FIGURE 7.9 Prepares food wearing cute carrot design pyjamas, in *planD* 플랜디.

goes about her daily household tasks. She does her housework carefully, diligently, with neatly positioned hands and an apron. In the narration provided, she makes statements like "This will give me time to fully focus on my child when she returns home", which promote her diligence, commitment, and focus upon motherhood and wifery. She doesn't talk about business, politics, or her views on the world – her concern is carefully organising her home and presenting every aspect in a way that is demonstrative of her love and care. Even the small towels are gently and decoratively handled.

FIGURE 7.10 Hamimommy wears an apron while folding towels decoratively. This is narrated by text that is again centred on her traditional gender role.

*Loli:* We see similar images of a wife/mother with folded laundry in *Kim Ji-young: Born 1982*, only the context is not one of idealisation, but the potentially unhappy realities associated with the role. These connotations, however, are not appropriate for the branding of the vlogs, which make a profit by idealising these practices, and making housewifery beautiful.

We also see a similar style of image in *Mr Housewife* (2005), although it is of the delicate and proud preparation of food by Ji-man for his wife and child. He carefully places the chopped chillies that he has crafted into flowers on top of the bulgogi to decorate. These little touches and extra efforts resemble those emphasised in the homebody and housewifery vlogs.

*EonniCafe* 언니카페, who has 2,090 subscribers, is a lesser-known wife/mother vlogger, who even uses dressing in the apron as an element of her videos.[9] She gives considerable focus to the apron. Like previous examples, she rarely shows her face. Her apron is often shown instead of her face, even when there is no task underway, showing that inactivity and an apron simply filling the camera frame is prioritised over any other activity. Usually, shots like this would feature the vlogger's face as they talk, but instead, for Korean lifestyle vloggers like *EonniCafe* 언니카페, the apron represents the woman, and her voice is replaced with text narrating what she thinks, feels, and is doing. One might even argue that the silencing of their voice, modesty towards displaying their faces, and focus on symbols of diligence like the apron, are an extension of neo-Confucianism into the branding and marketing of products within the female sphere of K-content, such as vlogs.

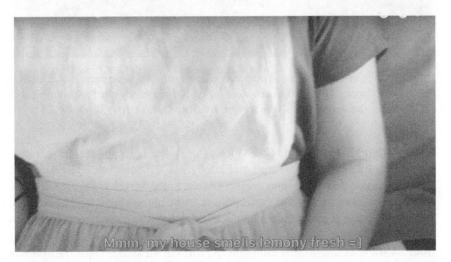

**FIGURE 7.11** As the written text narrates her words, the camera only shows her apron, in *EonniCafe* 언니카페.

FIGURE 7.12   Repeated shots of the back of the apron are used, even though it prevents the viewer from seeing the task at hand, in *EonniCafe* 언니카페.

FIGURE 7.13   Even when the meal preparation is over, the women remain in the 'kitchen space' (the work area) watching on as the men conduct ancestral rites in the 'living room' (the serving area), in *Kim Ji-young: Born 1982*.

*EonniCafe* 언니카페 begins her video by dressing in her apron. The narrative text reads 'Just had our breakfast and hubby has left for work'. The narration of this situation combined with dressing in the apron makes a clear association between traditional roles and these objects – the apron (hers) and work (his). The apron is then given considerable focus, both temporally and cinematographically. The whole process of dressing in the apron shows the straps, the ties from a variety of angles that highlight the form of an apron. Once the apron is tied, she cleans the house and cooks, all the time wearing her apron as a proud uniform.

Repeated shots of the back of the apron are used, emphasising its traditional style, and it's clearly a priority as this view actually prevents the viewer from seeing the task at hand. It shows just how important the image of the apron is in the branding of the vlog.

Location, as explained earlier, was incredibly important in neo-Confucian Korea, and the concepts of 'inside people' (wives) and 'outside people' (husbands) is still found remaining in the little customs and preferences of Korean people today. Of the signifiers that remain of these inner and outer spaces, which are often the kitchen ('work area' for women) and the living area or dining table ('reserved for men and elderly to rest'), the apron is undeniably one of women and the female space. One only needs to observe the Korean language to see the continued use of terms that express this concept of inner and outer people. For instance, address terms for one's wife such as *annae* (아내) 'inside person' or *jibsaram* (집사람) 'house person' are still used today, especially the latter. Kiaer and Kim explain "just like *annae*, *jibsaram* literally translates as 'house person', implying that women's sole duties lie within the house; hence showing that even in contemporary society, women are still being segregated from the outside world."[10]

Korean women are also physically shown occupying and being restricted to these spaces. There is no longer male and female segregation as there was during the Joseon period; however, some families still observe this tradition during family holidays like *Chuseok*, and even in those families that do not, women are implicitly commanded to occupy the same spaces, creating a continuation of the segregation that formally appears to have been dispersed with. For instance, cooking happens in the kitchen. If a woman is cooking all day, then she is in the kitchen all day. Meanwhile, the men who do not cook but rather play games, drink, and rest in the living room all day.

In *Parasite*. Mrs Kim is only seen wearing an apron once, after firing her housekeeper, which is telling of the power of wealth in Korea. This aligns well with her incompetence at housewifery, made clear in her husband's complaints about her inability to keep house or cook. Her lack of commitment to the role is clear visually also, as she wears her apron over expensive clothes. In contrast, Ji-young's clothing is simple and modest, with her hair roughly tied back, and no makeup.

Mrs Park even appears physically uncomfortable amidst her attempts at chores. This is visible in her tense, rushed movements, in a scene of domestic chaos. Her plastic glove-wearing also connotes this. Partly because in an earlier scene, Mrs Park puts plastic gloves on to pick up a pair of women's underwear brought home by her husband after he found them in his car. They believe the underwear belong to a woman seduced by Mr Park's driver. Mrs Park, who is disgusted, agitatedly puts her disposable gloves on to examine it and drop it in the bin. Given that her husband had already passed it directly to her, the putting on of her disposable gloves seems pointless, and therefore largely performative to demonstrate her separation of herself from the 'dirty' artefact, as she believes herself to be too delicate and sophisticated to touch it.

## Peeling fruit

Our final object is more of an action, with an object that we have already discussed: the peeling of fruit. This is much like the wearing of aprons, as can be seen in *Kim Ji-young: Born 1982*.

*Loli:*   When Ji-young's sister-in-law arrives, Ji-young is immediately asked by her mother-in-law to prepare more fruit. They need to create the fantasy of the daughter-in-law serving them – the perfect *Chuseok* – for their daughter to see too.

*Jieun:*   It is very rare for men to peel fruit, and most likely the daughter-in-law's job, if there is one. In fact, a woman's incompetence at peeling an apple, for example, can result in a telling-off. The reason this is such a common image is because we most commonly eat fruit after meals. With this has come its own customs, which like everything else reflect the hierarchy in every social dynamic that the activity takes place within.

Peeling fruit is a strong enough signifier of womanhood that it is wielded to show feminine stereotypes in films and other forms of media. *Mr Housewife* is just one example. As well as wearing an apron, Ji-man also peels fruit while his wife, the breadwinner, eats the fruit and relaxes. This same protocol is shown in *Kim Ji-young: Born 1982*, and again it is used in the context of womanhood, only this time to emphasise its expectations in Korea.

FIGURE 7.14  Jin-man peels the fruit, and his wife eats the fruit, in *Mr Housewife/Quiz King*.

FIGURE 7.15   (a) Ji-young peels the fruit, and (b) her in-laws eat the fruit while relaxing, in *Kim Ji-young: Born 1982*.

## Notes

1   Li, Yuhui. 2000. "Women's Movement and Change of Women's Status in China." *Journal of International Women's Studies*, 1(1), pp. 30–40. https://vc.bridgew.edu/jiws/vol1/iss1/3
2   *Naehun* (내훈) 'Admonishment for Women' was written by Queen Sohye, also known as Queen Mother Insu, in 1475.
3   "At its most basic, the *schenti* was a rectangular piece of cloth, wrapped around the hips and held in place by tucking one end into the tightly wrapped waist or by wearing a tied belt." https://fashionhistory.fitnyc.edu/schenti/

4 Kim, Ju Hee, and Keum Seok Chae. 2018. "Characteristics of Korean Apron Examined through the East and West Costume History." *Journal of the Korean Society of Clothing and Textiles*, 42(1), pp. 159–171. https://doi.org/10.5850/JKSCT.2018.42.1.159

5 한국의 고구려 벽화 안악 3호분에도 여성이 흰색 앞치마를 두르고 주방일을 하는 모습이 그려져 있는데, 4세기에 그려진 이 모습이 현재 주방의 모습과 매우 유사하며, 앞치마의 형태와 사용 목.

6 Daily Cleaning Routine to keep the house clean | Housework Motivation VLOG 🖌 | Home Cooking Recipes: www.youtube.com/watch?v=uN80NoAOzzE&t=866s

7 Plan:D | Holiday of a homebody. Groceries and making snacks: www.youtube.com/watch?v=YqPFuu43w0U

8 Daily Cleaning Routine to keep the house clean | Housework Motivation VLOG 🖌 | Home Cooking Recipes: https://www.youtube.com/watch?v=uN80NoAOzzE&t=866s

9 Clean with Me Using Homemade All Purpose Cleaner | Housewife in Korea SILENT VLOG #9 | Pinay in Korea: www.youtube.com/watch?v=pPEPfdwcVoo&t=622s

10 Kiaer, Jieun, and Loli Kim. 2021. *Understanding Korean Film; A Cross-Cultural Perspective*. London: Routledge.

# 8

## KINGDOM

Our final chapter looks at words and objects of the Joseon through the lens of *Kingdeom* (킹덤) 'Kingdom' (2019). The Joseon era is a key component of *K-* because many popular period K-dramas are set then, and echoes of the Joseon dynasty still exist in contemporary Korean society. Therefore, this book really wouldn't be complete without a chapter on K-content that depicts the period. Joseon period K-dramas have been a key part of the K-Wave on-screen and have brought Korean historical objects and words into the lives of people around the world, stimulating the rejuvenation of these objects, and their uses and meanings. *Kingdom* in particular has stimulated the exploration of Joseon objects and was the first Korean Netflix Original.

Directed by Kim Seong-hun, *Kingdom* is a blended genre television series, best summed up as a period pandemic horror. Set in the 16th century, in a fictional Joseon, *Kingdom* follows Crown Prince Lee Chang, as he investigates the mysterious illness that has befallen the King. He becomes caught up in a deadly epidemic, while simultaneously trying to prevent his political opponents from seizing the throne. In a recent interview with *The Hollywood Reporter*,[1] Kim explained that although the series is known by many as a zombie series, the affliction of these "zombies" is actually meant to be a plague and is loosely based on a plague that did in fact take place during the Joseon period. In a record made in the 19th century in the *Annals of the Joseon Dynasty*, it is recorded that "In the fall, a mysterious disease began to spread from the west, and in ten days, tens of thousands of people died in Hanyang." Since all the goings on were recorded in these records, and the king was not permitted to read or alter it, they are considered reliable historical records.

DOI: 10.4324/9781003203230-8

## Opening scene

We have grouped our first three objects together, having selected them from the opening scene of the first episode of *Kingdom*. Their combination is purposeful in constructing inferences of the narrative to come, but not necessarily for non-Korean viewers. Since the montage is entirely constructed using visual objects, it demonstrates their significance in the way the K-Wave is being consumed on-screen.

The scene is a montage of shots of clothing, headdress, wafting incense, and acupuncture being performed on an unknown body. The scene is object focused. With no narrative or context appearing beforehand, we are provided with an ideal scenario to explore objects that are meaningful and implicative.

### *Dragon*

We begin with the dragon insignia. During the montage, we are given glimpses of dragon symbolism carved into the *sangtugwan* (상투관) (a crownlike topknot cover that was used to cover only the topknots of the king or crown prince) and on the robes worn by the unknown character. The king, crown prince, and sons of the crown prince were the only ones allowed to wear this type of robe and headdress. The robe, called *gollyongpo* (곤룡포) or *yongpo* (룡포), meaning 'dragon robe', was worn while performing official duties, e.g., when the king conducted state affairs, when the crown prince took lessons in the Confucian classics, when the son of the crown prince was studying.[2]

The dragon was a symbol of the king, depicted on a badge called *yongbo* (용보). The king's *yongbo* was round and embroidered with a dragon with five claws, while the crown prince's *yongbo* had a four-clawed dragon, and the crown prince's son's

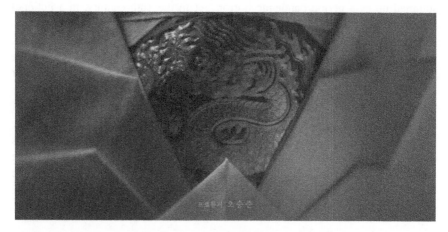

FIGURE 8.1   A glimpse of the dragon on the king's robe, in *Kingdom*.

robe was square and embroidered with a three-clawed dragon. The dragon's appearance changed with the times too. For example, founder of the Joseon, King Taejo (1335–1408), wore a *yongbo* with an S-shaped flying dragon with claws that appear in vigorous movement, and so symbolise the dynamicity of the time. King Yeongjo's (1694–1776) *yongbo*, however, depicts a dragon who is looking straight ahead with its five claws exposed. This was said to signify a stable rather than dynamic energy.

The Ming dynasty of China first introduced the dragon robe to Korea in 1444, in the 26th year of King Sejong's reign. It then assimilated into Korean custom after the Ming dynasty collapsed, with Korea's own style gradually being incorporated into its design. When *Gojong* became emperor, the robe, which had been red prior to this, was changed to gold.

Today, however, *hanbok* with dragon insignia is not reserved for Korean kings, crown princes, or their sons. It can be purchased online – both in sizes for adults and children – at a variety of major online stores – and in its accessibility, and at times misinterpretation, it is associated more generally with the *hanbok* of K-dramas among non-Koreans.

*Loli:*  "Korean" dragon insignia is also purchasable beyond *hanbok*, such as on t-shirts, mugs, and even embroidery kits with which you can embroider your own. Products, like the dragon badge embroidery kits, are sold by Korean sellers on Etsy; however, Korean dragon design products come from a variety of locations. I have frequently observed multiple regions featured in the keywords of a product title, such as "Korean Chinese dragon". Sometimes, it feels like the mention of an item being Korean or the Korean Wave is used to market East Asian products in general.

### Glutinous rice in the mouth

Rice now becomes our object again, only this time uncooked glutinous rice in the mouth, which has a different purpose and meaning in Korea and a different transmission in *K-*. The glutinous rice in the mouth is one of the most informative shots in the opening scene, implying to Korean viewers that the person wearing the dragon robe is dead, and likely seeming strange to non-Korean viewers. This action is part of the funeral procedure of inserting rice, beads, jade ornaments, or coins into the mouth of the deceased person.[3] This custom is known as *banham* (반함), and the items placed in the mouth are believed to be food or money for the deceased to use on their journey to the underworld, thus wishing them prosperity.

This footage, combined with the implicature beforehand that this man is the king, tells Korean viewers in the opening scene that the king is dead. For those unfamiliar with Korean culture, however, who this is and what is happening might not be clear at all. The glimpse of a red robe with dragon insignia, the golden dragon topknot cover, and the mouth filled with rice could be misinterpreted as

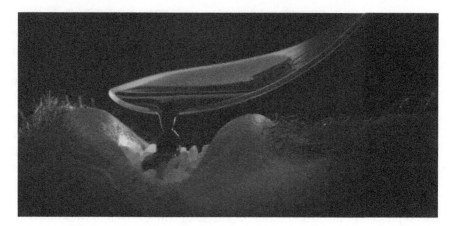

FIGURE 8.2   The king's mouth is filled with glutenous rice, and something unusual is being poured into the rice, in *Kingdom*.

medicinal or as a part of the preparation of a dead body in general. While this may not lead to the adoption of these burial rites outside of Korea, like how Korean traditional dress has influenced fashion and inspired cosplay trends, rice is again emphasised as crucial to Korean identity.

### Three ties

Before we present our next object, we will touch more on Korean burial rites, which involve multiple indigenous and adopted ideologies. Like *banham*, the burial rites of Korean and Western cultures are vastly different. Even between East Asian regions that have practices that bear some cultural similarity, burial rites are different. A traditional Korean funeral includes both Confucian customs and centuries of indigenous shamanism.

*Jieun:*   In Confucian tradition, mourners of the deceased are expected to mourn for 3 years, during which *Jesa* (제사) ceremonies must be performed by the eldest son and daughter-in-law. *Jesa* is a ceremony in which one's ancestors are memorialised, held usually on the anniversary of the person's death. This is a key part of Confucian burial rites because it is an expression of filial piety. Women are expected to cry, as this demonstrates the value of the deceased. Meanwhile, men are expected to remain calm and not to cry, demonstrating their self-control.

*Loli:*   Then in shamanism, there are offerings and prayers, often using music. The aim is to appease the spirits so they may allow the deceased to pass over to the afterlife with ease.[4] Scenes of shamanism like this aren't rare in K-films and K-dramas. For instance, if we return to *Pachinko* for a moment, you may recall that in the opening scene, Sunja's mother visits a shaman because she believes her children are dying young because her blood is cursed. We see images of shamanism appear often in K-films and K-dramas. Non-Korean viewers may simplify these shamanic ceremonies as being Korean magic, rather than being able to appreciate just how intricately woven shamanism is in Korean culture even today.

Koreans who practice Buddhism may also perform Buddhist burial rites, though we see this less in films set in the Joseon period, as Buddhism was outlawed by the government who wished to replace it with Confucianism. One example is a ceremony called *sasipgujae* (사십구재). Held while the deceased's spirit is believed to have not yet entered the afterlife, the ceremony signifies the ending of the Buddhist mourning period of 49 days, following which the deceased can completely cross over into the afterlife, and the bereaved family can also return to their everyday life.[5] K-films like the *Sin Gwa Hamkke* (신과함께) 'Along With the Gods' franchise, which is based on Joo Ho-min's webtoon *Along with the Gods*, shares this aspect of Korean burial rites with non-Koreans. In fact, the franchise has been incredibly successful with the first film *Along with the Gods: The Two Worlds* (2017) being the third highest-grossing film in South Korean film history in May 2019.[6] The films tell the interconnected stories of paragons, who are escorted to the afterlife by three guardians, who proceed to defend them in seven trials over the course of 49 days, in order for the paragon to be granted reincarnation and the guardians to be given credit towards their own reincarnation. The film was shot as one but presented in two parts, and a third film was announced to be in the works in 2019.

The objects that concern us here are the three vertical ties that are made to hold the shrouds around the body, which is a part of the practices and rituals of bathing and shrouding the body of the deceased, called *yeomseup* (염습). After shrouding,

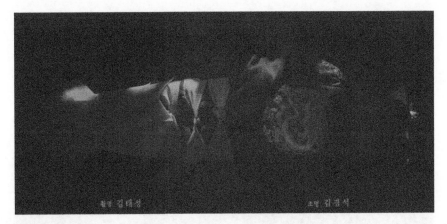

**FIGURE 8.3**   Three fabric ties and the dragon insignia centralised on the body within the camera frame, in *Kingdom*.

cloth ties are used to fasten the shrouds in place, using three vertical ties and one horizontal tie, all of which have their ends tucked in.[7] We see something similar in *Kingdom*, although only the lower half of the king appears to be shrouded in the full shot of the body, and there is no horizontal tie from head-to-toe shown explicitly. This could be a decision made to expose the dragon insignia on the robe of the body, to create the implicature that this is the body of a deceased king. It could also have been a practical measure, with the king being partially in the process of being de-shrouded. Since the opening scene is a montage, with no information given prior, a great deal is left to the imagination. Whatever the intention, there are three clearly distinguishable ties, and it can be argued that there is no other inferable cultural purpose than to signify that the body was or is in the process of being shrouded.

### Gat

During the Joseon period, like language and behaviour, there were strict restrictions on what one could wear, and it was all dependent on one's status. Neo-Confucianism made Korean society so sensitive to relations that one had to be clear about who they were in all respects, to ensure smooth interpersonal relations. This created an even greater gap between high officials and the poor, just as it clearly distinguished position, age, and gender. Hats played an important role in this, and there was an array of styles for the job. Not wearing any hat at all would reflect a person's poverty.

Of all the hats, the *gat* (갓) is the hat that has become synonymous with K-content, especially among non-Korean fans. No wonder, perhaps, that the word *'gat'* is also used as a general term for Korean traditional hats in Korea, despite each hat having its own name. Further, this interest isn't at all new, but rather widely spread thanks to social media. Foreign travellers who travelled to Korea during the Joseon period were equally fascinated by the *gat*. Broughton,[8] for instance,

FIGURE 8.4   The Crown Prince wearing the *gat*, in *Kingdom*.

described the *gat* worn by people of higher status as "large black hats, with high crowns, manufactured with a strong gauze, not unlike horsehair, very stiff and strong. They tied them under the chin; and these hats, serving as umbrellas, were three feet in diameter." Adams[9] proclaimed these black hats to be a symbol of the Joseon.

There are ample opportunities to observe the *gat* in *Kingdom*, and in all Joseon period K-dramas. The fascination surrounding the *gat* is perhaps because of the extent to which it plays a role in distinguishing Korean traditional clothing from that of other East Asian regions. From a layman's perspective, clothes in China, Japan, and Korea at this time were wrapped and tied rather than buttoned, and both men's and women's clothing was composed of long robes. Hairpins and decorations, similarly, were common forms of apparel among these regions. Thus, it was the hats of Korea, especially the wide-brimmed, black *gat*, that stood out, differentiating Korean fashion from what Western travellers at the time could and did often generalise.

It is not only fans' awareness and interest in the *gat* that has grown. Interest in this object in the West has been building since much earlier in the Korean Wave. This is evident when one considers the simple principle of supply and demand. The *gat* found its way into modern high fashion in the West as early as 2011, in fashion designer Carolina Herrera's spring 2011 ready-to-wear collection, which was inspired by the traditional clothes of Korea and botanical plates collected in the 18th century.[10] When asked how she came up with the idea of including *gat* and *hanbok* as elements in her designs in an interview with *Korea JoonAng Daily* newspaper, Carolina Herrera answered: "I saw books and paintings (about them) and I investigated the library because I wanted to have that special look. I loved the hats. I translated them for the shows because I thought they were very elegant. It was a very successful collection, and it is one of my favourites."[11]

Thanks to period K-dramas like *Kingdom*, the traditional *gat* is also being sold at major online stores, including Amazon, eBay, and Etsy. The link between the market for the *gat* and *Kingdom*, for instance, is demonstrated in how keywords in the title of the hats sold online often include '*Kingdom*', as well as in the *gat* memes inspired by *Kingdom* that were created and shared among fans on social media platforms, such as Twitter.[12] Many of the memes reference the variety of *gat* and their flamboyant designs. This is especially significant if we consider that *The Korea Times* reported that *Kingdom* was the most mentioned K-drama on Twitter globally in 2021.[13]

## Feather

Before we move on from the *gat* entirely, we briefly touch on another related object – the feather, which is worn on several Korean traditional hats as a symbol of status. The aristocracy wore hats decorated with a peacock feather. Adams (1870: 129) reported that on his travels, the Joseon men who wore hats "distinguished by a single peacock's feather" had an air of superiority over others about them. 'He also suggested that peacock feathers were granted to those in good favour with the Chinese emperors as it is a similar style to the head dressings of Chinese nobility.[14]

### Hairpins and hairpieces

Continuing on the subject of headwear, the traditional Korean hairpin or *'binyeo'* (비녀) is our next object.

Online sellers of these items tag their products with "*Kingdom*" and "k-drama", and other dramas like "Mr Queen" referring to the K-drama *Cheorinwanghu* (철인 왕후) 'Mr Queen' (first released in 2020); making clear their target market includes K-fans. Sellers also include keywords like "*hanbok*" in a multitude of ways, such as "Korean Royal *hanbok* jewelry"; then "Korean kingdom *binyeo* for *hanbok* jewelry", "kingdom jewelry *hanbok* hair stick". *Hanbok* is a familiar word, so describing the hairpin as "*hanbok* jewellery" or "*hanbok* hair stick", is a means of engaging with non-Koreans. Koreans know the word *binyeo* which is also included on three occasions; however, consideration of potential non-Korean interpretations of the products show that they are targeting non-Koreans too.

Like the last example, which featured images from K-dramas, this hairpin is marketed with multimodal references to *K-* too. The seller provides several images for each item, including different angles of the items, and the models in different poses, using a variety of gestures. Although the seller doesn't use K-Wave in the keywords of the title, this is expressed gesturally by the finger heart gesture in the images. The finger heart gesture is a beacon for K-fandom, and for these sellers it is as powerful as literally spelling out 'K-Wave' in the title. The finger heart's presence confirms that consumers are not buying traditional Korean culture but rather buying K-ness.

FIGURE 8.5   The evil queen with her hairpin, in *Kingdom*.

## Beef pancakes

Our next object is one that contributed to food trends: beef pancakes. *Yukjeon* (육전) or *soegogi jeon* (쇠고기전), as it is known is Korea, is thinly sliced beef that has been lightly battered in flour and egg and pan-fried. It is a popular side dish, served with rice and other side dishes. There is a humorous scene in *Kingdom*, in which the crown prince playfully confronts his bodyguard over stealing from his dessert dish to feed his pregnant wife. He then asks the bodyguard to embark on a dangerous mission for him, tempting him with beef pancakes when he falters.

K-fandom not only talked about the beef pancakes referenced in the scene on Twitter, but even created humorous comic-style artwork based on it. These memes riff on the humour of how beef pancakes are thought to be 'so delicious' by the

**FIGURE 8.6**   Then, when there is no final mention from the Crown Prince of the beef pancakes, his bodyguard raises the subject to confirm that they are still available, and humour is conveyed to the audience, in *Kingdom*.

man that he would risk his life to get them for his wife. However, as we discussed in Chapter 2, beef has always been of high status in Korea due to there being very limited land for raising cattle. Beef pancakes were not an easy thing to come by, especially for a lowly bodyguard. Therefore, this is less about deliciousness or the dish being a favourite, but rather about its rarity and value and subsequently the beliefs attached to it ('this is expensive, so if you feed this to your wife you are feeding her the best').

It wasn't the first time that beef pancakes had become a subject of interest either. The same interest had to be stirred before by the K-drama *Baegirui Nanggunnim* (백일의 낭군님) '100 Days My Prince' (2018). In *100 Days My Prince*, beef pancakes are the favourite food of the lead character, Lee Yool, who likes the dish so much that in one scene he even considers eating one that has fallen on the floor.[15] Scenes like this have led to beef pancakes becoming a subject of discussion among K-fans.

As we have demonstrated throughout our objects, the simplicity and accessibility granted by the combination of the K-Wave on-screen and social media is fundamental to how these objects come to express *K-*. *Maangchi*, who is famous for her Korean cooking videos and recipes reaffirms this. She provides a Korean beef pancake recipe for English speakers on her website, which is also linked to her YouTube channel, and other forms of social media.[16] This demonstrates the accessibility factor that objects and words able to become elements of *K-* typically have. In the video, *Maangchi* says that making beef pancakes is "very easy, simple recipe, but delicious". *Maangchi* specifies that beef pancakes are a side dish for rice, or a component of a Korean lunchbox. After preparing the pancakes, she then shows how to prepare the lunchbox, which she explains is called *Dosirak* (도시락). This is the next layer of snow that gathers around the snowball.

*Loli:*   Beef pancakes become a gateway for the concept of *dosirak*, and for the idea that a beef pancake belongs in a Korean lunchbox. Meanwhile the *dosirak*, which can be made of numerous Korean foods, becomes associated with beef pancakes. This is how hybridity can be seen developing organically and purposefully through online social media, demonstrating the snowball effect. The people creating the content – everything down to the word choice in the titles they give to their videos, the things they talk about, and how they present the K-content that they are delivering – can influence how hybridity develops and what snowballs and how.

## Clown

Our final object in this book is very much related to Korean film and television, because it is the humble beginnings of the acting profession in Korea: the clown. This is not, however, the clown most Western viewers will call to mind, with their painted faces, wigs, and slapstick comedy. In ancient Korea, clowns were equivalent

**FIGURE 8.7**   Clowns, in *Kingdom*.

**FIGURE 8.8**   Famous scenes of clowns from *The King and the Clown*.

to the modern-day actors. Often observed in period K-dramas and K-films, these people were considered no different from slaves by Korean society. They would perform short plays or acts involving acrobatics or tightrope walking, often donning traditional masks. They may be mistaken for performers, and their status may be lost in translation, but this is where low status and a lack of respect for actors originates. When we see K-pop stars and famous actors, such as Lee Jung-jae from *Squid Game*, attend award shows on television, it is hard to imagine this. It isn't that celebrities in Korea aren't idolised. However, idolisation is accompanied by a touch of stigma that can't quite be washed away by modernity or Westernisation.

*Loli:* The brief images of clowns performing their act while nobles attend a feast in *Kingdom* is representative of those seen across period K-films and K-dramas, though it doesn't give their lives focus, so the connotations of low status and hardship are lost. Korean masks like those worn by clowns can even be bought online. However, the film *Wang-ui Namja* (왕의 남자) 'The King and the Clown' (2005) is one of the few films that really gives focus to the lives of clowns, adding traditional depth to interpretations of this traditional art entirely as *K-*.

## Notes

1 Lee, Hyo-won. 2019. "Netflix's Korean Original Series 'Kingdom' Puts a Zombie Spin on the Historical Epic." *The Hollywood Reporter.* www.hollywoodreporter.com/author/lee-hyo-won/

2 The *Encyclopaedia of Korean Folk Culture* defines *gollyongpo* (袞龍袍) as "Everyday royal robe worn by kings, crown princes, and sons of crown princes with a jade belt (okdae), royal hat (ikseongwan), and black boots (heukpihwa)". See https://folkency.nfm.go.kr/en/topic/detail/6866 for more on *gollyongpo*.

3 See the online *Encyclopaedia of Korean Folk Culture* for 'Insertion of grains into the mouth of the deceased (飯含)': https://folkency.nfm.go.kr/en/topic/detail/140

4 In *Hanyang Kut: Korean Shaman Ritual Music from Korea* (2002) the author Maria K. Seo writes that shamanism is "alive and well in Seoul in a rich tradition reaching back to the Chosôn Dynasty (1392–1910), the capital of which was Hanyang (now Seoul)."

5 S*asipgujae:* The 49th day memorial rite in a Korean Buddhist funeral: https://folkency.nfm.go.kr/en/topic/detail/199

6 Naver. 2018. [Official] 'With God', 'International Market' beaten . . . 2nd most popular movie of all time. https://entertain.naver.com/ranking/read?oid=382&aid=0000625070

7 The *Encyclopaedia of Korean Folk Culture* explains the process of shrouding the body: "After bathing and dressing the body of the deceased, it is moved on to a piece of pre-pared cloth. A silk-lined garment is rolled up and placed under the head instead of a pillow, and the two ends of the silk garment are rolled up to fill the gaps above the shoulders. Other old clothes are used to fill the gaps between the legs and beside the legs, and to cover the body. The body is then wrapped in the cloth on which it is placed, the feet first, then the head, then the left side and right side. The body is wrapped with the straps, vertically first and then horizontally, with the ends tucked in rather than knotted. Lastly the body is covered with a cloth.": https://folkency.nfm.go.kr/en/topic/detail/310

8 Broughton, William Robert. (1804) 2000. *A Voyage of Discovery to the North Pacific Ocean . . . Performed in His Majesty's Sloop Providence, and Her Tender, in the Years 1795, 1796, 1797, 1798.* Seoul: Gyeongin munhwasa.

9 Adams, Arthur. (1847) 2000. *Notes from a Journal of Research into the Natural History of the Countries Visited During the Voyage of H. M. S.* Samarang, *Under the Command of Captain Sir E. Belcher, C. B.* Seoul: Gyeongin Munhwasa.

10 Vogue's coverage of Carolina Herrera's spring 2011 ready-to-wear collection: www.vogue.com/fashion-shows/spring-2011-ready-to-wear/carolina-herrera

11 *Korea JoongAng Daily*'s 2013 interview with Carolina Herrera: https://koreajoongang-daily.joins.com/2013/06/03/features/Fashions-first-lady-focuses-lens-on-Asia/2972536.html

12 SAU-SIEGE. "Kingdom on Netflix has the greatest hats... oh, and zombies." https://twitter.com/SAU_SIEGE/status/1105089254844219392/photo/1

13 Dong Sun-hwa Reported. "'Kingdom' Most Mentioned Korean Drama on Twitter." www.koreatimes.co.kr/www/art/2022/10/398_316391.html

14 Adams, Arthur. (1847) 2000. *Notes from a Journal of Research into the Natural History of the Countries Visited during the Voyage of H. M. S.* Samarang, *Under the Command of Captain Sir E. Belcher, C. B.* Seoul: Gyeongin munhwasa.

15 Drama Milk. 9 October 2018. "Drama Food: Beef Pancakes from 100 Day My Prince! (Yuk-jeon or Soegogi-jeon." www.dramamilk.com/drama-food-beef-pancakes-from-100-days-my-prince-soegogi-jeon-쇠고기전/

16 Maangchi's recipe for Korean beef pancakes: www.maangchi.com/recipe/soegogi-jeon

# APPENDIX 1

## Sources

**TABLE A1** Television show sources

| Television show title | First released |
|---|---|
| *Naui Ajeossi* (나의 아저씨) 'My Mister' | 2018 |
| *Miseuteo Seonshaein* (미스터 선샤인) 'Mr Sunshine' | |
| *Ojingeo Geim* (오징어 게임) 'Squid Game' | 2021 |
| *Kingdeom* (킹덤) 'Kingdom' | 2019 |
| *Bijeongsanghoedam* (비정상회담) 'Abnormal Summit' | 2014 |
| *SKY Kaeseul* SKY (캐슬) 'Sky Castle' | 2018–2019 |

**TABLE A2** Film sources

| Film title/s | Year of release |
|---|---|
| *Gisaengchung* (기생충) 'Parasite' | 2019 |
| Naranmalssami (나랏말싸미) 'King of Letters' | 2019 |
| *Sin Gwa Hamkke* (신과함께) 'Along with the Gods' | 2017 |
| *Sado* (사도) 'The Throne' | 2015 |
| *Miseuteo Jubu Kwizeuwang* (미스터 주부퀴즈왕) 'Mr Housewife'/'Quiz King' | 2005 |
| *Wang-ui Namja* (왕의 남자) 'The King and the Clown' | 2005 |
| *Sampoganeun gil* (삼포가는 길) 'The Road to Sampo' | 1975 |
| *82 Nyeonsaeng Gim Jiyeong* (82년생 김지영) 'Kim Ji-young: Born 1982' | 2019 |
| Hanyeo (하녀) 'The Housemaid' | 2010 |
| Hanyeo (하녀) 'The Housemaid' | 1960 |

**TABLE A3** Vlog sources

| Vlog name | Video title | Video link |
|---|---|---|
| Hamimommy | Daily Cleaning Routine to keep the house clean ǀ Housework Motivation VLOG 🧹 ǀ Home Cooking Recipes | www.youtube.com/ watch?v=uN80NoAOzzE&t=866s |
| '꿀주부 Honeyjubu' | What I Ate In A Week/ Easy Korean recipes to make  Honeyjubu A diligent daily life that starts at 5 in the morning | www.youtube.com/ watch?v=Qp_3MitNwBY&t=5s  www.youtube.com/ watch?v=3vdd2_qiMWQ&t=327s |
| EonniCafe언니카페 | Clean with Me Using Homemade All Purpose Cleanerl Housewife in Korea SILENT VLOG #9 ǀ Pinay in Korea | www.youtube.com/ watch?v=pPEPfdwcVoo&t=622s |
| PlanD플랜디 | Plan:D ǀ Holiday of a homebody. Groceries and making snacks  Plan:D ǀWeekend VLOG, all by myself. Home-made meal after the grocery. Life with simple home-cook | www.youtube.com/ watch?v=YqPFuu43w0U&t=366s  www.youtube.com/ watch?v=DiAdFCr-tKY&t=69s |
| Maangchi | Maangchi's recipe for Korean beef pancakes | www.maangchi.com/recipe/soegogi-jeon |

# INDEX

Note: Page numbers in *italics* indicate figures and those in **bold** indicate tables.

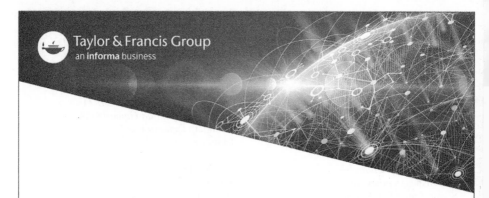